Modern Approaches to Traditional Elements

Japanese Design

Wisteria Flowers in Byodo-in Temple: © Katsuhiko Mizuno 2001

Modern Approaches to Traditional Elements

Japanese Design

Edited by DesignEXchange

A DEX BOOK

Copyright © DesignEXchange Company Limited.

Published in the United States in 2001 by
Gingko Press Inc
5768 Paradise Drive, Suite J
Corte Madera, CA 94925
Phone:(415) 924-9615 Fax:(415) 924-9608 USA
e-mail: books@gingkopress.com
http://www.gingkopress.com

Published in Europe in 2001 by
Gingko Press Verlag GmbH
Hamburger Strasse 180
22083 Hamburg, Germany
Phone:(040) 291425 Fax:(040) 291055
email: gingkopress@t-online.de
http://www.gingkopress.com

Published in Japan in 2001 and distributed worldwide except USA, Canada, and Europe by
DesignEXchange Company Limited.
BR Takanawa 3-12-8 Takanawa
Minato-ku Tokyo 108-0074 Japan
Phone:81 3 5798 0216 Fax:81 3 5798 0212
e-mail:intl@dex.ne.jp
http://www.dex.ne.jp

ISBN 1-58423-081-9

Publisher: Masanori Omae
Text, Research, Editing, and Book Concept: DesignEXchange Company Limited
Editorial Cooperation: Nostalgic Japan
Hotel Okura
Michiko Takagi
Template design: Fontage
Book Design + CD-ROM production: Katsuya Moriizumi
Production, Co-edition control, and Marketing: Rico Komanoya
English Translation: Moriya Translation Office (Toshio Moriya, Rory Baskin and John Bryan)

Manufactured in Hong Kong by Everbest Printing Company Limited.

First Printing, 2001

TABLE OF CONTENTS

Preface

The Edo period of Japan was a period in the history of art that not only reflected development in paintings but also revealed a remarkable advancement in the arts and crafts. As the economic situation of merchants and city people became more prosperous there emerged a strong desire to enjoy life on top of the daily necessities of food, clothing and shelter. Hand crafted goods materialized that were given different and varied designs and decorations, and that were different to the handicrafts of the existing aristocratic and samurai culture of the time.

In the field of fabric coloring the Yuzen dyeing process was completed about the end of the 17th Century, and kimonos that looked really as gorgeous as the traditional folding screen had become very popular. In the field of receptacles or crockery, the technology of colored picture porcelain that had been brought into Japan from Korea, produced such porcelain pottery as Imari pottery, Ironabeshima (or colored Nabeshima ware) , and Kutani pottery. The brilliance of this pottery was matched by colored porcelain developed in Kyoto and represented by Kyo-yaki.

In the architectural design of the Edo period, such things as the pictures on fusuma doors, derived from the artists of the period and the detail that came to characterize their colorful works, complemented the architectural design of red-light districts and merchant's houses. ("Fusuma" are room partitioning sliding doors made of paper and decorated with pictures). These ornaments of art peculiar to Japan have not stayed in Japan and the influence bestowed in various ways on paintings and ornamental art in far away Europe, is not difficult to envisage. In ornamental handicraft goods, architectural design and posters that emerged all over Europe due to the popularity of the new art artisan's movements such as "Art nouveau", "Jugendstil" and "Style moderne" etc., we can see the influence of the ornamental art of the Edo period on the decorative design and the methods of expression.

In the history of arts and handicrafts in Japan, we would not be exaggerating if we said that since the Meiji period, when almost every field of Japanese culture was westernized, the field of ornamental art from the flamboyant Edo period was chased down as representative of Japan's culture, and was to become the part of Japan's traditional rituals and ceremonies that would live on.

Yuzen-sai Miyazaki who was a sensitive individual representing the Genroku period (1688-1704) and the originator of the Yuzen dyeing process, thought like this: "A new cultural era cannot be born unless we study the magnificence of past traditions and flavor them with the freshness of the periodicity of our time."

We should not shut the magnificent ornamental art that blossomed in the Edo period away into art history or traditional ceremonies, but have it resuscitated in the current world of computerized design so as to release us from the stereotypes and enable us to create new designs representative of Japan today.

Chapter 1

Modern Approaches to Traditional Design Elements

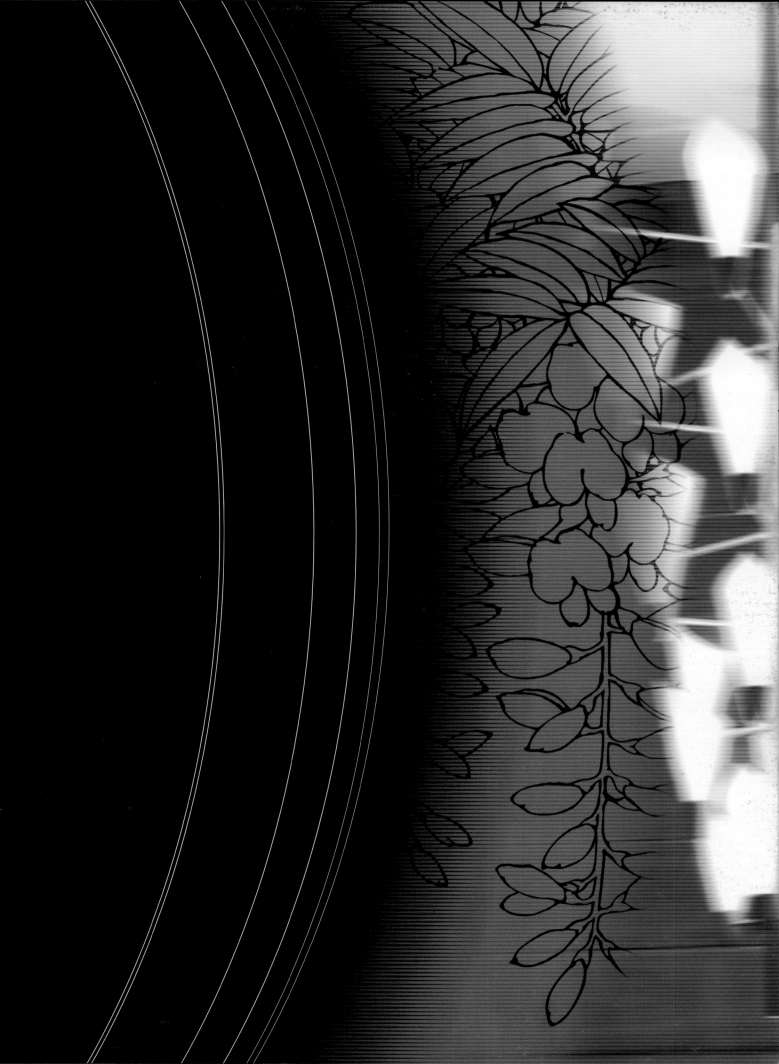

Floor Lamp

Material: Patterned design on Warlon sheet,
stainless cut-leaf etching + Acrylic multi-layers
Dimensions: 1800mm X 490mm

Cherry Blossoms

Up until the late Heian period, Japanese Apricot had
been the one of the representative design patterns.
However the Cherry blossoms that were not grown in
the Mainland China then established its firm position as
the main element in the Japanese design. This relates to
the fact of the period that the Japanese culture started
the first and unique step by setting free from the strong
influence from the Chinese culture. The beauty of
dropping of Cherry blossom petals on the ground is the
symbol of the aesthetic mind deep stemmed in Japanese
people since then.

Floor Lamp

Design: Nostalgic Japan
Production: Muromachi Art
Material: Kyo-yuzen on Warlon sheet
Dimensions: 700h X 300w X 300d

Above: New variation of the Yuzen-style swimming suits

Right: 1972 Munich Olympics Japanese women's swim team - swimming suits

Production: Mizuno Corporation Limited

**Cherry Blossoms
Folding Screen**

Design: Muromachi Art
Production: Muromachi Art
Material: Lacquer on Japanese
cypress
Patterned design on aventurine
lacquer

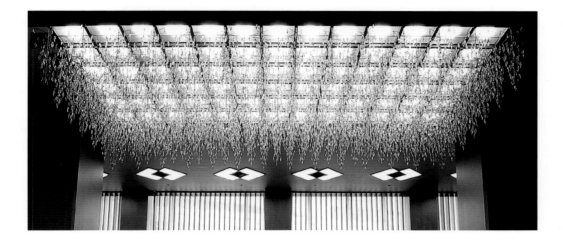

HOTEL OKURA
Wisteria chandelier in the entrance lobby to the
grand banquet hall.

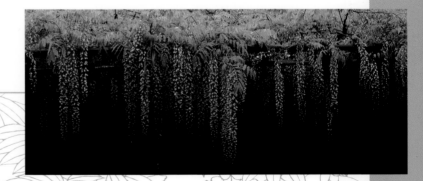

FUJI (Wisteria Flowers)

In ancient Kyoto the festival of wisteria Flowers
was held each year at the Fujitsubo House (House
of Wisteria Flowers) within the Imperial Court.
The flower that has graced the landscape every
early summer has been transferred by the artists on
to handicraft pieces and dyed fabrics.

HOTEL OKURA
Wisteria ceiling lighting in the entrance lobby
to the grand banquet hall.

Wall Lighting

Design: Fontage
Production: Nostalgic Japan
Material: Tie-dye on silk,
stainless cut-leaf etching + Acrylic multi-layers
Size: 800 mm x 1,200 mm

AKIKUSA
(Autumn Flowers)

The motif of autumn flowers expresses the sadness about the vanity and impermanence of worldly things that lies in the depths of the Japanese senseof aesthetics. Japanese bush clovers, Japanese pampas grasses, Chinese bellflowers, fringed pinks, autumn bellflowers, patrina scabiosaefolia, and other plants that do not have any brilliance express this sadness. We can see the modest shape of their natural growth as they nestle together, and we can feel the philosophical beauty.

Hoitsu Sakai's "Summer and Fall Grasses Folding Screen" is a representativeof these works.

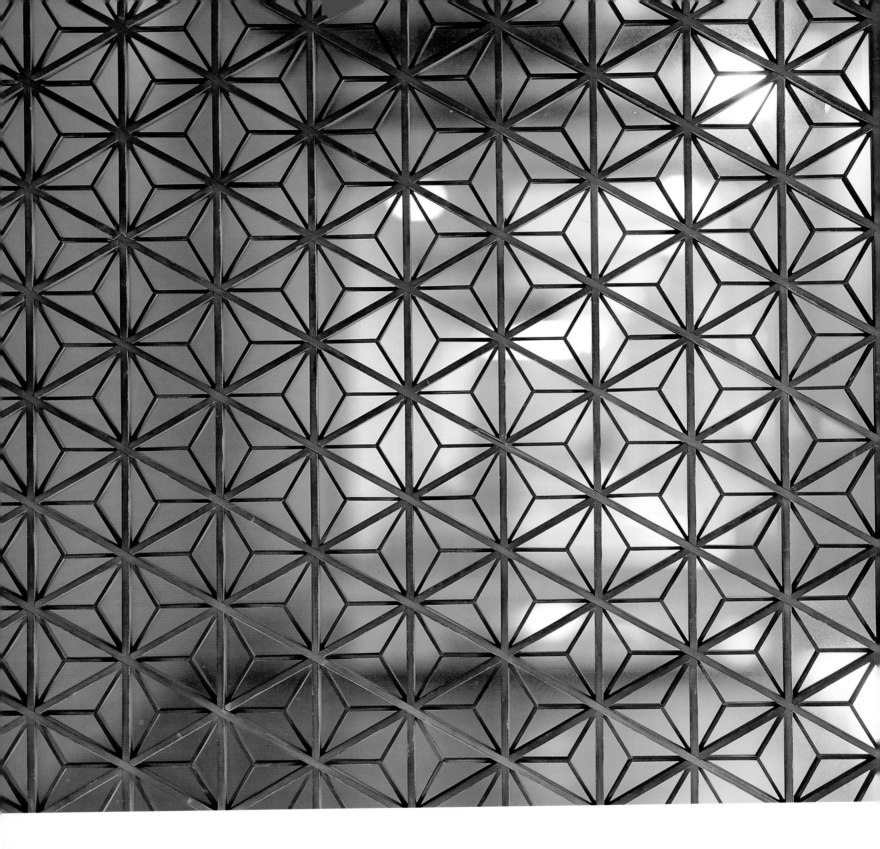

Left: HOTEL OKURA ASANOHA-MON screen, lobby-floor

Right: George Nakashima floor and table lamps

Production: Sakura Seisakusho Inc.

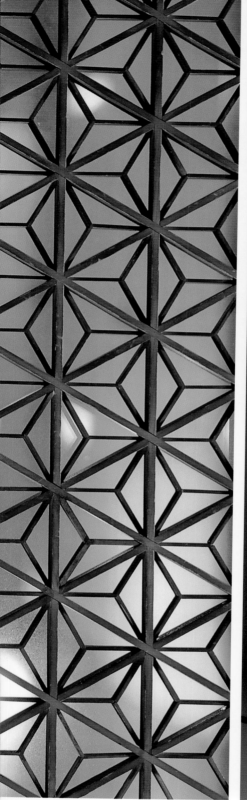

ASANOHA-MON
(Hemp Leaves Patterns)

Put six equilaterial triangles together to form a hexagon, and you have a perfect hemp leaf pattern. We use it on transom windows and sliding doors. You may see dyed hemp leaves on ladies' handbags and other personal articles. The usage of the pattern is very wide, hence its great importance.

This pattern is feminine. It is often used on obi, juban (kimono undergarment) and kimono. We associate ASANOHA-MON with Omiwa and Yaoya Oshichi, favorite kabuki heroines. It also reminds us of Ukiyoe yukata (informal summer kimono).

HOTEL OKURA ASANOHA-MON screen, main lobby

Stream

This makes a pattern with an image of running water as the title says. The pattern of running water is combined with various motifs. This representative pattern of running water expresses the nature of Japan's four seasons.

HOTEL OKURA
Kyokusui-no-Niwa (The Winding River Garden)

During the Heian Period the Imperial Palace in Kyoto held on the third day of March each year a festival (of dolls) called the Banquet of the Winding River. Men of letters stood on the banks of a winding stream. As sake cups floated down-stream, each man was expected to compose a poem before he picked up a cup to drink from it.
This was the game played of the banquet. The room garden in Hotel Okura is a replica of the ancient Winding River Garden.

Counter

Counter main body
Design: Fontage
Production: Nostalgic Japan
Material: Steel-pipe frame + wooden stand
Size: 2200 mm (W, extensive) x 850 mm (H) 430 mm x 1,200 mm

Panel
Design: Fontage
Production: Nostalgic Japan
Material: Tie-dye on silk with gold-leaf inlay + coated grass on the reverse
side/Pearly tie-dye on polyester textile + coated grass on the front side
Size: 2200 mm (W, extensive) x 850 mm (H) 430 mm x 1,200 mm

KIRIHAKU (Cut-leaf)

Silver and gold leaf are cut into small pieces and pasted on with glue or lacquer. There is also a decoration technique that scatters powdered leaf ("sunago"). They are used to produce Japanese paintings, colored paper, folding fans, lacquer ware, and other items.

Mug

Design: Ichiro Tsuruta
Production: Sakurai
Direction: Nostalgic Japan
Material: New bone china
Method: Transcription

Sake cup

Design: Ichiro Tsuruta
Production: Sakurai
Direction: Nostalgic Japan
Material: Brass
Method: HVS Transcription

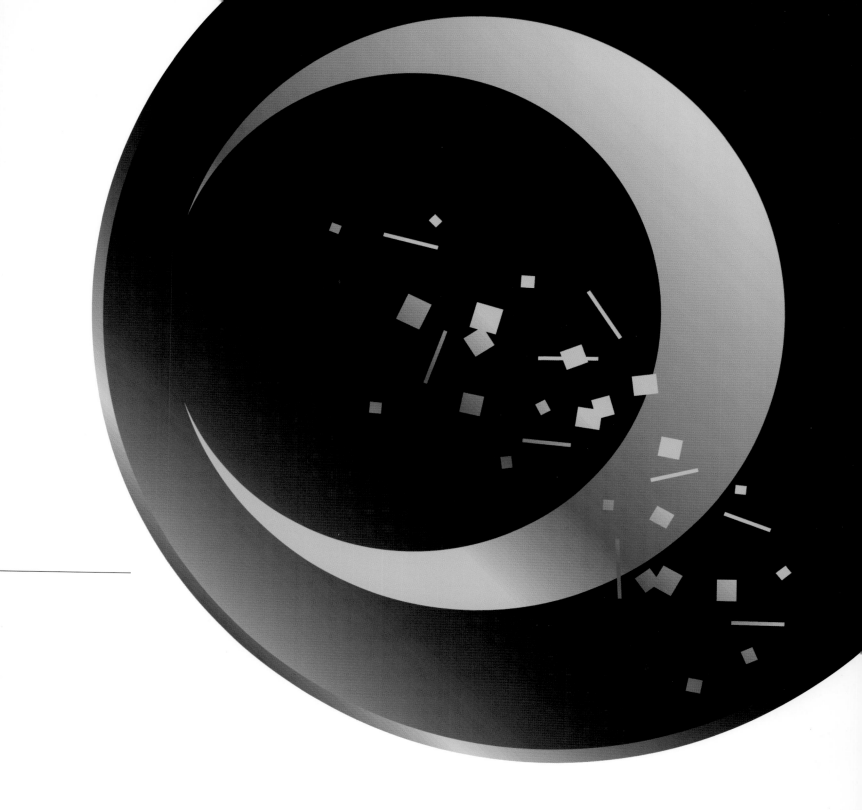

Half Moon Tray

Design: Ichiro Tsuruta
Production: Sakurai
Direction: Nostalgic Japan
Material: Resin (tau) clear coating
Method: transcription

HOTEL OKURA
Mural of the grand banquet hall,
Heian-no-ma

Patterns of "The Poems of Thirty-six Poets"

The beauty of the cursive characters in black on the glistening background defines description. The whole panorama reveals to us the elegant world of the Heian nobility. The great murals of Heian-no-ma are a reproduction of the format, designs and patterns, colors, methods, and materials of the thirty-seven volumes of the thirty-six poets, and recreate for us the glamor of the Heian court.

One of the patterns found in the poetic collection is called Suminagashi. It describes rushing water in a stream. This can be done by one of two methods: by drawing with a brush or dropping black Indian ink on a wet sheet of paper and then transferring it to another sheet. What you see on the walls of the Seiryu-no-ma is a blowup of a photographic impression of Suminagashi done at Hotel Okura. We believe that we succeeded in recreating the classic beauty of Suminagashi.

KOSHI (The latticework)

The lattice is a simple openwork structure of crossed stripes of wood. The typical Japanese latticework has been seen in shutters and ceiling of shrines and temples. The shutter was later replaced by the sliding door. It was hinged to the lintel and pushed up to open.

Hotel Okura made it their basic policy to revive the classical and indigenous architectural art. Under this policy the original Japanese latticework has been used extensively. A typical example is the lattice shutters seen on the walls of the grand banquet hall. You will observe latticework in two straight lines, making a sharp contrast with the colorful murals. They also serve to embrace the huge hall.

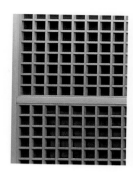

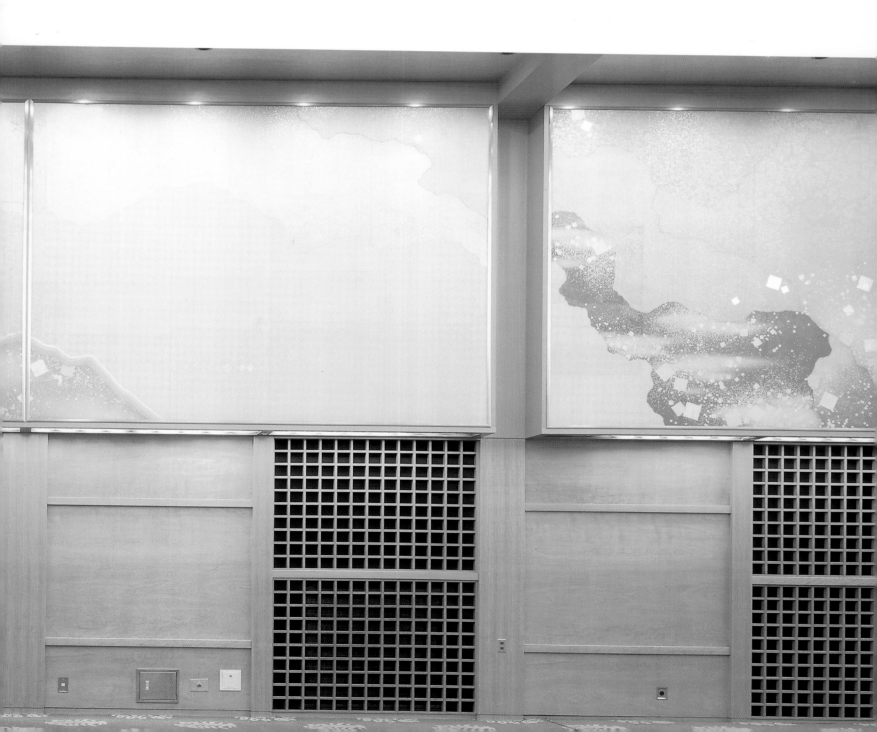

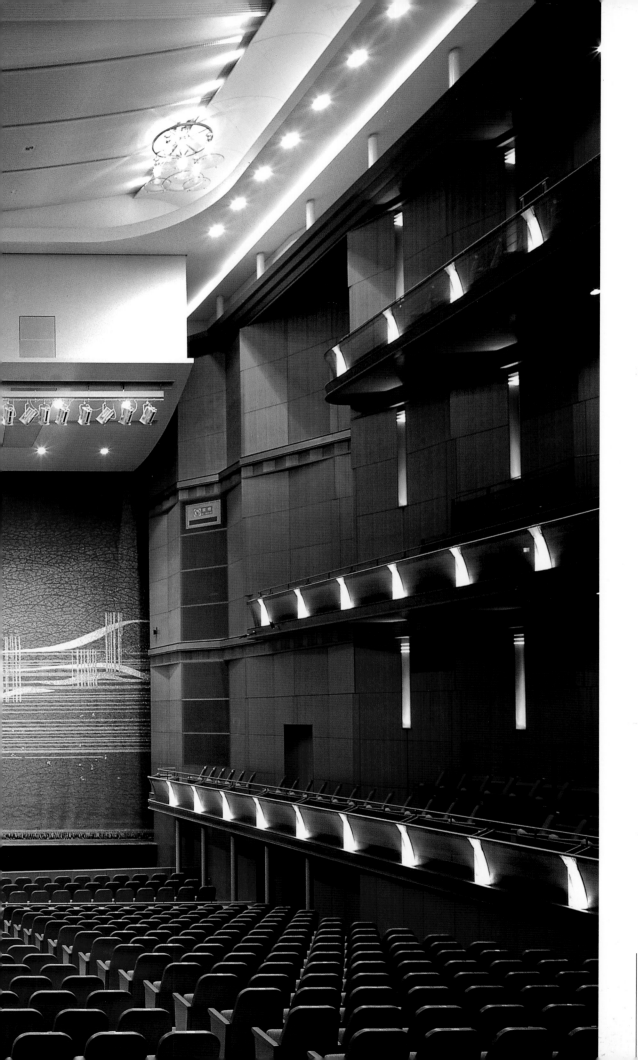

Drop Curtain

Kumamoto Castle Cultural Center
Design: Keisui Yamazaki

Drop Curtain

Kumamoto Castle Cultural Center
Design: Keisui Yamazaki

OHGI (The Fan)

The fan made its first appearance in Japan during the Heian period (A.D. 794-A.D. 1185). Today you will find two general types of fan: the flat (HI-OHGI) and the folding (SENSU).

OHGI is also called SUEHIRO which literally means "wider toward the end". Thus the name is a good omen, and as such the fan is often used as a good luck symbol for individuals and businesses. The fan as a design has been used both singularly and plurally. You see the single fan as a family emblem. During the Muromachi Period (A.D.1341-A.D.1568), an activity called NAGASHI OHGI-literally, floating the fans down the river—came into being, and another decorative design named after it has captured popular acclaim.

Wooden screen of the banquet room, Suehiro-no-ma.

HOTEL OKURA
Wooden screen of the banquet room, Suehiro-no-ma.

HOTEL OKURA
Flower arrangements on the
checker pattern

ISHIDATAMI-MON
(The Checker Pattern)

Among the many geometrical patterns, the checkers are the simplest and the most stable-appearing. We call this pattern ISHIDATAMI-MON, because the checker board looks like a stone pavement (ISHIDATAMI).

During the Edo Period Ichimatsu Sanokawa, a Kabuki actor, wore a checkered Hakama (Japanese skirt), and the pattern became popular overnight. In fact, the other name of ISHIDATAMI-MON is ICHIMATSU-MON. In old times the checker pattern was also called Arare, or hailstones, and during the Heian Period, a more elaborate pattern was created by superimposing the shape of cut-away section of the melon upon the checkboard.

Ceiling pattern of the banquet room, Seiran-no-ma.

Various Approaches

Using traditional shapes to approach to the modern-day products

Coffee spoon

Design: Ichiro Tsuruta
Production: Sakurai
Material: 18-10 stainless steel
Transcribed on gold plated HVS

**Hot pot
Mouth Pad
Snowboard**

Design: Fontage

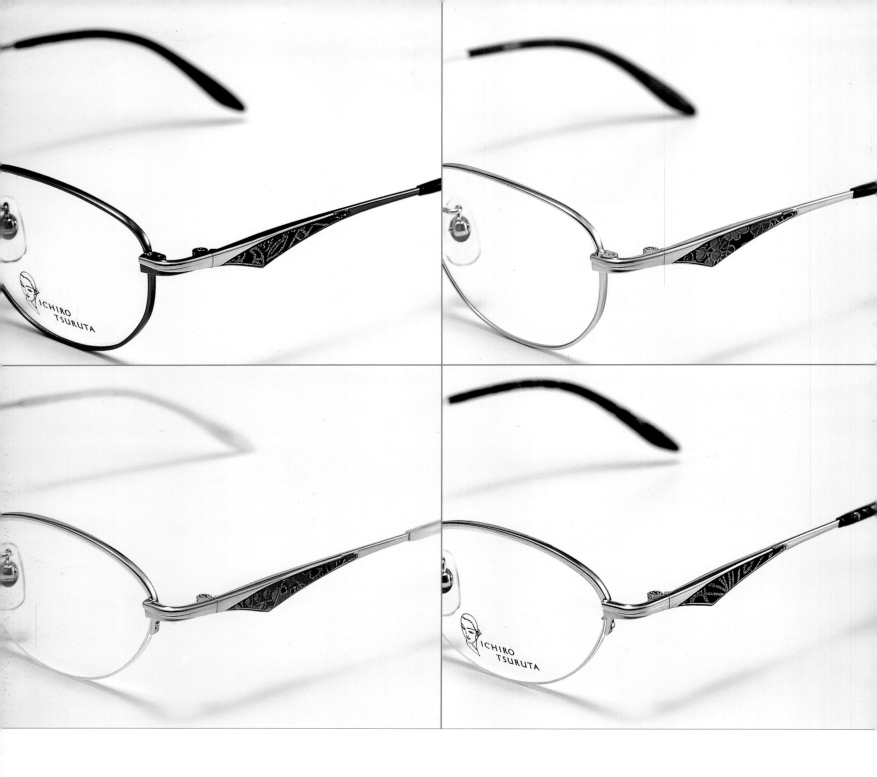

Eyeglasses

Design: Ichiro Tsuruta
Manufacturing: Folx
Material: Titanium and Japanese paper
Size: 53 mm x 135 mm/55 mm x 135 mm
Production: Fontage

Sofa

Design and Direction: Ichiro Tsuruta
Production: Nostalgic Japan
Material: Wooden frames with Nishijin textile and silver inlay
Size: 2300 mm (W) x 820 mm (H) x 850 mm (D)

Using traditional shapes to approach to the modern-day products

Various Approaches

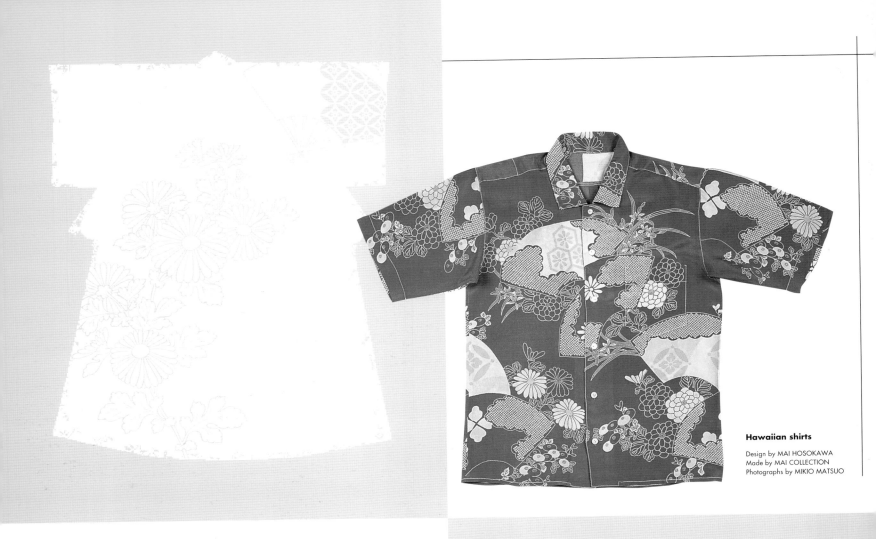

Hawaiian shirts

Design by MAI HOSOKAWA
Made by MAI COLLECTION
Photographs by MIKIO MATSUO

Hawaiian shirts

Design by MAI HOSOKAWA
Made by MAI COLLECTION
Photographs by MIKIO MATSUO

Hawaiian shirts

Design by MAI HOSOKAWA
Made by MAI COLLECTION
Photographs by MIKIO MATSUO

Hawaiian shirts

Design by MAI HOSOKAWA
Made by MAI COLLECTION
Photographs by MIKIO MATSUO

Hawaiian shirts

Design by MAI HOSOKAWA
Made by MAI COLLECTION
Photographs by MIKIO MATSUO

Hawaiian shirts

Design by MAI HOSOKAWA
Made by MAI COLLECTION
Photographs by MIKIO MATSUO

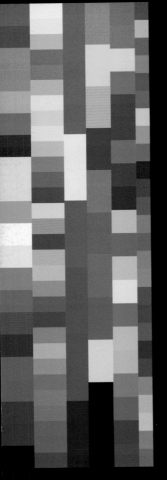

Chapter 2
Japanese Traditional Colors of the Era

CMYK percentage described in the color palettes in this chapter is for reference only.

AYA
Color scheme with flowery changes.

Nara Era: A.D.562-793

The style of the Orient and some countries west of China looks like imperial properties of Shosoin Treasure House. This is an expression of magnificent varied color made possible by the development of techniques from that area.

Name	C	M	Y	K
Akaneiro	C 30	M 98	Y 79	K 0
Enjiiro	C 53	M 98	Y 84	K 0
Shuiro	C 0	M 87	Y 93	K 0
Shinshu	C 24	M 69	Y 69	K 0
Ouni	C 0	M 62	Y 91	K 0
Trubami	C 50	M 70	Y 83	K 0
Kuriiro	C 86	M 93	Y 95	K 10
Kihadairo	C 7	M 8	Y 87	K 0
Kariyasu	C 0	M 13	Y 96	K 0
Oudoiro	C 20	M 48	Y 94	K 0
Nyuhaku	C 6	M 3	Y 11	K 0
Byakuroku	C 22	M 0	Y 22	K 0
Rokusho	C 72	M 26	Y 66	K 0
Hanadairo	C 91	M 41	Y 22	K 0
Aiiro	C 100	M 46	Y 10	K 10
Koiai	C 100	M 73	Y 45	K 10
Suouiro	C 43	M 91	Y 66	K 0
Kodaimursaki	C 68	M 78	Y 41	K 0
Shikoniro	C 85	M 95	Y 74	K 0
Kokimurasaki	C 90	M 93	Y 77	K 0
Sumiiro	C 93	M 81	Y 84	K 80

Heian Era: A.D.794-1191

The elegant charming colored arrangements reflect the brilliant culture that centered around the nobles.

Elegant, graceful, and courtly. **MIYABI**

Sakurairo	C 0	M 16	Y 11	K 0
Ikkonzome	C 0	M 22	Y 13	K 0
Koubaiiro	C 0	M 56	Y 33	K 0
Beniiro	C 18	M 98	Y 64	K 0
Karakurenai	C 6	M 97	Y 77	K 0
taikou	C 20	M 43	Y 39	K 0
Kuchinashiiro	C 0	M 18	Y 69	K 0
Yamabukiiro	C 0	M 31	Y 95	K 0
Kouiro	C 13	M 23	Y 39	K 0
Chojiiro	C 18	M 33	Y 57	K 0
Kourozen	C 45	M 58	Y 79	K 0
Kuchibairo	C 62	M 68	Y 95	K 0
Hiwadairo	C 77	M 86	Y 95	K 0
Wakanaeiro	C 21	M 0	Y 92	K 0
Moegiiro	C 41	M 0	Y 98	K 16
Fukamidori	C 100	M 50	Y 96	K 0
Seijiiro	C 48	M 0	Y 42	K 5
Kamenozoki	C 46	M 7	Y 19	K 0
Asahanada	C 70	M 23	Y 19	K 0
Nakahanada	C 88	M 54	Y 49	K 0
Kokihanada	C 100	M 65	Y 25	K 0
Asagiiro	C 88	M 10	Y 24	K 0
Fujiiro	C 37	M 35	Y 0	K 0
Ouchi	C 50	M 50	Y 0	K 0
Futaai	C 66	M 65	Y 14	K 0.
Kikyoiro	C 63	M 58	Y 0	K 0
Shion	C 61	M 61	Y 34	K 0
Kakitubatairo	C 58	M 83	Y 0	K 0
Suouiro	C 43	M 91	Y 66	K 0
Ebiiro	C 85	M 85	Y 60	K 0

HARI

As the tension is not loosened it becomes tight.

Kamakura Era: A.D.1192-1333

The rational spirit of the samurai, their will reflected in their lives, intelligence, and essence are a colored sensation. The arrangement of the colors reflects their moral spirit that respects the uprightness and warns against the weakness at the time.

Name	C	M	Y	K
Akaneiro	C 30	M 98	Y 79	K 0
Kokihi	C 30	M 98	Y 89	K 0
Shiroiro	C 8	M 12	Y 29	K 0
Miruiro	C 78	M 63	Y 94	K 0
Tokusairo	C 90	M 56	Y 89	K 0
Ruriiro	C 98	M 68	Y 0	K 0
Tetsukon	C 100	M 78	Y 64	K 31

Muromachi Era: A.D.1334-1573

The charm is seasoned with patina and you can feel the joy of the deep stillness. Somber colors controlling the vividness and the achromatic color of the Indian ink painting. There is a beauty of refined simplicity.

Elegant, graceful, and courtly. SABI

Name	C	M	Y	K
Hiiro	C 5	M 92	Y 84	K 0
Yamabukiiro	C 0	M 31	Y 94	K 0
Hiwairo	C 16	M 0	Y 99	K 15
Senzaimidori	C 93	M 73	Y 100	K 0
Botaniiro	C 28	M 91	Y 0	K 0
Suouiro	C 43	M 91	Y 66	K 0
Tobiiro	C 58	M 68	Y 84	K 0
Nibiiro	C 75	M 65	Y 74	K 0
Ginnezu	C 23	M 14	Y 17	K 0
Keshizumiiro	C 48	M 28	Y 24	K 84
Sumiiro	C 93	M 81	Y 84	K 80

AYA
The gorgeously shining beauty.

Momoyama Era: A.D.1574-1602

There is a fresh and lively wild beauty. The color of various splendid colors is emphasized by the gold that competes for splendor and brilliance.

Name	C	M	Y	K
Beniiro	C 18	M 98	Y 64	K 0
Shojohi	C 11	M 98	Y 89	K 0
Yamabukiiro	C 0	M 31	Y 94	K 0
Matsubairo	C 78	M 41	Y 94	K 0
Konjo	C 100	M 73	Y 4	K 0
Gunjoiro	C 98	M 83	Y 0	K 0
Umemurasaki	C 43	M 82	Y 52	K 0
Shikoniro	C 84	M 95	Y 73	K 0
Kuromurasaki	C 93	M 90	Y 87	K 10
Shiracha	C 26	M 25	Y 43	K 0
Sabishu	C 50	M 81	Y 76	K 0
Akagouiro	C 19	M 32	Y 46	K 0
Tonokoiro	C 8	M 15	Y 38	K 0
Karacha	C 52	M 66	Y 97	K 0
Rikyushiracha	C 28	M 22	Y 46	K 0
Sabiseiji	C 44	M 10	Y 37	K 0
Sabiasagi	C 75	M 39	Y 49	K 0
Sabinando	C 88	M 50	Y 54	K 0
Senzaimidori	C 96	M 71	Y 99	K 0
Senzaicha	C 77	M 78	Y 97	K 9

Edo Era: A.D.1603-1867

This fashion of colors came from the commoners, not the samurai and the nobles. It is the fashion the commoners like. It includes elegant simplicity and flexibility.

A chic feeling and clean appearance that is polished and attractive. **IKI**

Name	C	M	Y	K
Enjiiro	C 53	M 98	Y 84	K 0
Kakiiro	C 0	M 55	Y 66	K 0
Benikabairo	C 40	M 88	Y 94	K 0
Kakishibuiro	C 37	M 63	Y 64	K 0
Kuriume	C 62	M 82	Y 89	K 0
Bengarairo	C 48	M 80	Y 92	K 0
Ukon iro	C 5	M 28	Y 92	K 0
Kitsuneiro	C 24	M 51	Y 92	K 0
Ginsusutake	C 64	M 64	Y 82	K 0
Kenpoiro	C 88	M 89	Y 94	K 24
Kogecha	C 78	M 78	Y 92	K 10
Rikancha	C 73	M 73	Y 94	K 0
Rokocha	C 50	M 53	Y 89	K 0
Mirucha	C 68	M 63	Y 94	K 0
Negishiiro	C 60	M 44	Y 61	K 0
Rikyunezu	C 61	M 37	Y 54	K 0
Nandonezu	C 91	M 63	Y 67	K 0
Nandoiro	C 100	M 58	Y 54	K 0
Noshimeiro	C 94	M 52	Y 39	K 0
Koiai	C 100	M 73	Y 45	K 10
Edomurasaki	C 84	M 89	Y 48	K 0
Hatobanezu	C 59	M 45	Y 39	K 0
Fukagawanezu	C 40	M 22	Y 24	K 0
Sakuranezu	C 24	M 25	Y 24	K 0
Umenezu	C 51	M 59	Y 49	K 0
Botannezu	C 63	M 72	Y 54	K 0

Chapter 3
Yuzen Textiles and Patterns

Drawing

The artist's work is finally accomplished when it is drawn on silk fabric with a writing brush.
Sometimes it is delicate. Sometimes it is audacious.
Let's understand the origin of this art.

Sketch the design using dayflower juice extract on white silk fabric, then proceed to put a tracing paste made from steaming rice, on top of the sketch lines.

In reality, the dyeing process involved in creating the exquisite picture pattern worlds of Yuzen is complicated.

First, decide on the design motif, then roughly draw the outline pattern onto the silk.

The process will pass through many stages in the following order.
(1) Shita-e (the design) (2) Nori-oki (the placing of resist paste) (3) Aobana-otoshi (removing the design lines)
(4) Ji-ire (preparing the material by coating it with bean juice) (5) the Yuzen process (applying colors)
(6) Fuse-nori (layered pasting) (7) Ji-zome (dyeing the whole base except the pattern) (8) steaming (9) washing
(10) smoothing with steam (11) drying (12) finishing

Once the color and design are largely decided, and using the liquid dayflower extract (Aobana) that will disappear when heated, you proceed to sketch the design onto the white silk pieces that have been sewn together provisionally. This extract comes from one kind of dayflower produced in the Yamada region near Tokaido-Kusatsu and is made from a liquid extracted from its ultramarine colored blossom that blooms in midsummer.
Paste is traced in fine lines (itome-nori) on the design outline sketched in dayflower extract in order to prevent the dye from running. This is called "bo-sen." After you have completely finished placing the paste, but before applying the dyes, fix the paste well by sprinkling on bean juice . This enables any paste, which has softened to hardened again and allows you to measure and determine the density of the paste.

In order to allow the many hues and tints to surface, apply the vivid colors with a writing brush.
Apply color to the pattern portions using a small flat brush or a writing brush. From this point on the process is one that requires a proficient technique and the feeling of the artisan. Beginning with the preparation of dyes and colors, the coloring process is calculated and conducted by means of a number of subtle strategies such as using gradations of colors, shading, and overall contrast. Mistakes are not permitted.
Once you have applied color to the design, you can proceed to "ji-zome," or dyeing the background weave of the fabric. The cloth that is colored using a fawn's hair brush is put into a steam room to fix the color. It is then moved on to a water bath where it is washed. Gorgeous colors and hues become clear when the artisan makes the cloth swim about in the water. Sometimes the cloth is reeled up, and beaten over a wooden bench. By repeating this rough process over and over, excess foreign matter is washed out of the dyed cloth and it breathes a new life. If this process, that requires undivided attention, is repeated over and over, a mysterious world of colors emerges and so much beauty is created that it is impossible to put into words.

Dyeing

Dyeing is a long mind-boggling process that finally results in the appearance of brilliant colors.
It is like that special feeling you get in your heart and the excitement you confide in yourself when spring visits.

The delicate colorful expressions of Kata Yuzen (stencil Yuzen) are generated from layering coats of tracing paste that are mixed with dyes.
Yuzen techniques can be categorized as Hand-painted Yuzen and Kata Yuzen.
In Hand-painted Yuzen, we have various techniques such as itome Yuzen, and line-less Yuzen (itome-nori is not used), hand-painted Yuzen, tsuke-tate Yuzen (controlled concentration color is applied without using outlines), flowing dye Yuzen, Each one possesses its own special characteristics. On the other hand, Kata Yuzen that prints to fabric patterns using paper patterns, is characterized by a fine motif wholly inlaid and portraying delicate expression. Large numbers of the same pattern can be made at one time. This was largely made possible by the invention of tracing paste.
Tracing paste, a substance made from mixing dyes in placing paste, is spread evenly over the pattern paper placed on the cloth, using a wooden spatula known as a "koma-bera." Since the dyes are mixed into the paste, the pattern paper is changed according to the picture drawings many times for successive colors to be added. In this technique, the colors are fixed by steaming and soon after, when it is washed in water, the paste is removed leaving only the colors behind.

To decisively control the quality of the pattern, the craftsman consumes enormous amounts of nervous energy and time, finally embossing the motif that gives life to Kata Yuzen.

There are three stages in stencil paper creation of, namely, texture paper coating, layering, and engraving. Sheets of the highest quality texture paper, minogami (one type of Japanese paper washi), are coated with persimmon juice and stuck together by using hardened substance from smoked sawdust. These are divided into groups according to application, 2 layers, 3 layers, 4 layers etc. The thicker the paper the better when the patterns are being etched in roughly. The completed engraved pattern paper is moved to a dyeing table where dyeing work is carried out. After much varied and painstaking work, the job will be finished.

The fabric comes to life with repeated steaming, washing, smoothing with steam, and drying.

The coloring and dyeing process together with the hand drawn motifs and patterns brings a masterpiece of brilliance up to the surface.
To reach this point, the processes of steaming, washing, smoothing with steam and drying have to be repeated many times. As a result of these processes the vivid colors will rise up and new life will sparkle in the fabric.

Decorations

Finally, as a result of adding decorations, gold coloring and embroidery, a design is congealed in the fabric that is absolutely gorgeous and unbelievably magnificent.

The beauty abounds and sparkle begins with the artisans picture motifs.

Embroidery, gold coloring, and mother of pearl work.

Kimono is colored in the most gorgeous and luxurious way.

In addition to the magnificent manual techniques, in order to beautifully finish off the fabric, color is added from various clothes and ornaments of the Heian period. People have been charmed by such remarkably outstanding techniques as the embroidery patterns using colored thread and gold and silver thread, the extravagant use of gold for coloring and the use of beautiful mother of pearl with its mysterious gleam.

The embroidery of the pattern, carefully sewn section by section and stitch by stitch according to each motif, is work that requires much perseverance.

You can say its a technique that is familiar and suited to the sensitivity of Japanese who love delicate beauty, and, when two dimensional motif patterns take on a three dimensional flavor, a beauty overflows that cannot be put into words. In addition, we must not forget that gilding or the use of gold, is a technique that generates in the Japanese sense of beauty, a feeling of what is truly luxurious and gorgeous. Some methods included in this technique such as gold leaf, gold sprinkle, and impressed gold, are being used selectively in sections to bring to life and portray expressions of richness or balance.

In any case, we cannot say enough about the magnificence, the quiet beauty and attractiveness or the height of extravagance of kimono that is imparted by gold.

You will now touch on the crystallization of beauty which the sensitivity of the Japanese and their sense of beauty has given birth to.

Embroidery, the coloring of gold, and of course mother of pearl work.

The crystallization of charming beauty arising out of tasks that consume a mind-boggling amount of labor and free time is reflected traditionally and culturally in the kimono. The kimono and its exquisite coloring is as much a product of the Japanese landscape and its beautiful expressions of four seasons as the sensitivity of the Japanese people and their sense of beauty.

We are able to touch the richness of their inherited and continuing culture by enjoying the feeling of dressing in the kimono. Isn't that the real happiness that has been passed on to us Japanese?

Yuzen Templates

A diagonally cut trellis with wisteria on it strengthens the downward flight of the wisteria petals. This example marries concreteness and abstraction.

Wisteria Trellis
FUJIDANA

The background with cut-leaf pieces of gold lets us imagine the warm light of a spring field.

Violets
SUMIRE

P A R T S

P A R T S

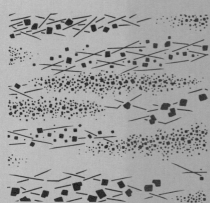

Narcissuses, also known as flowers in the snow, comfortably grow with a lattice pattern background. This presents a crisp image of early spring.

Narcissuses
SUISEN

Blossoms are blown away and scattered by the breeze. Sometimes the
single petals are scattered all over
the background.

Scattered Cherry
Blossoms

**SAKURA-
CHIRASHI**

Peonies

BOTAN

Showy peony blossoms look more
beautifully displayed in high-toned
geometric hemp leave patterns.

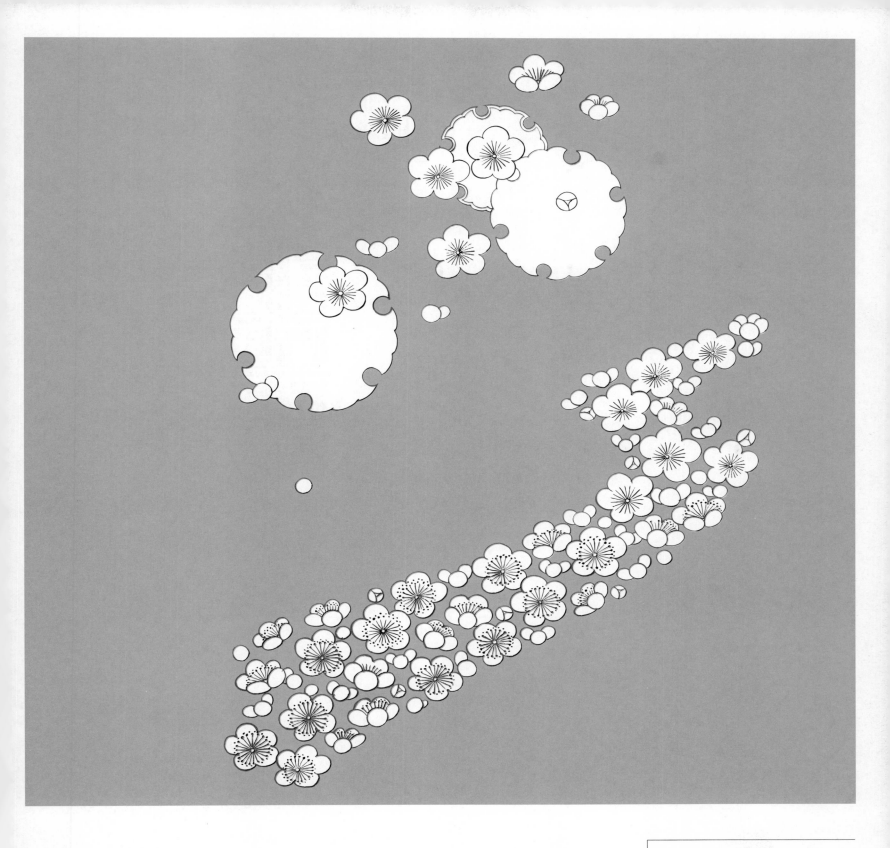

Japanese apricot blossoms in running water are on the bottoms of
kimonos and snow crystals designs
are on the shoulders. The disks are
designed from snow crystal.

Japanese
Apricot Blossoms
in running water
UME-RYUSUI

P A R T S

| PAGE:70 | FILE FORMAT:EPS | FILE NAME:57_Suisen.eps |

P A R T S

| PAGE:71 | FILE FORMAT:EPS | FILE NAME:48_Sakura-chirashi.eps |

   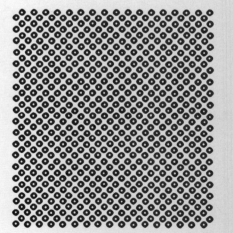

PAGE:72 | FILE FORMAT:EPS | FILE NAME:13_Botan.eps

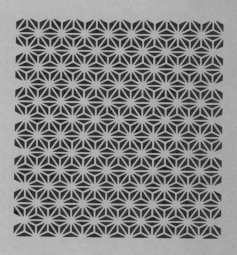

PAGE:73 | FILE FORMAT:EPS | FILE NAME:68_Ume-ryusui.eps

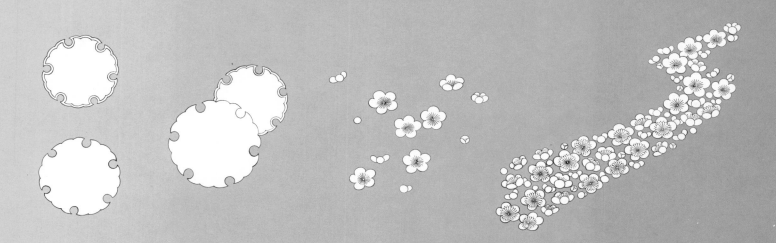

Cosmoses on the left side of the picture make the space on the right side even more extensive. Gradated silhouettes provide perspective for the picture.

Cosmoses
AKIZAKURA

PARTS

PAGE:76

FILE FORMAT:EPS

FILE NAME:09_Akizakura2.eps

A flurry of cherry blossom petals fall on a brook and this accent of spring is carried off into the distance. This is a moving scene in the spring.

PARTS

PAGE: 77

FILE FORMAT: EPS

FILE NAME: 21_Harukaze.eps

Spring Breeze

HARUKAZE

Drooping cherry tree blossoms create a stream from the top of the picture to the bottom. The direction of the stream makes us feel the presence of the empty space beneath the blossoms.

Drooping
Cherry Tree
Blossoms

SHIDARE ZAKURA

PARTS

PAGE:78

FILE FORMAT:EPS

FILE NAME:51_Shidarezakura.eps

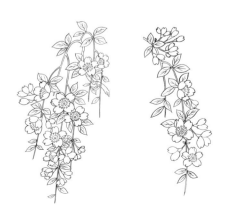

Cherry blossoms as a motif of spring have various charms of their own according to the kinds and periods. The direction of the stream of drooping cherry tree blossoms makes us feel the presence of the empty space beneath the blossoms.

PARTS

PAGE:79

FILE FORMAT:EPS

FILE NAME:44_Ohkabyobue-zu.eps

Cherry Blossoms
Folding Screen

**OHKA
BYOBUE-ZU**

This bold use of cherry blossoms in full bloom depicts a showy and brilliant spring scene.

Cherry Blossoms
SAKURA

This is a layout used for a painting on a folding screen. Full-blown cherry blossoms with the perspective of a misty background depict a mild spring day.

Blooming flowers
KAIKA-ZU

Rape Blossoms

NANOHANA

Overlaid images of rape blossoms remind us of a garden of rape blossoms in the spring.

This image of a wisteria trellis creates a three-dimensional effect by using empty space under the wisteria flowers.

Wisteria Flowers
FUJI

PARTS

| PAGE:80 | FILE FORMAT:EPS | FILE NAME:49_Sakura.eps |

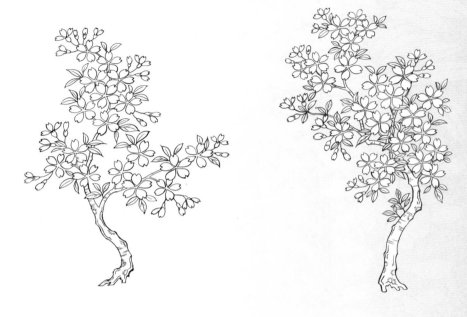

PARTS

| PAGE:81 | FILE FORMAT:EPS | FILE NAME:29_Kaika-zu.eps |

PARTS

PAGE:82 | FILE FORMAT:EPS | FILE NAME:41_Nanohana.eps

PARTS

PAGE:83 | FILE FORMAT:EPS | FILE NAME:14_Fuji.eps

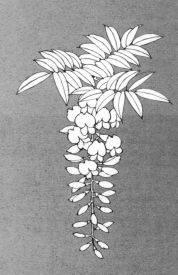

Wild dandelions growing together are effectively depicted with cut-leaf gold.

Dandelions
TANPOPO

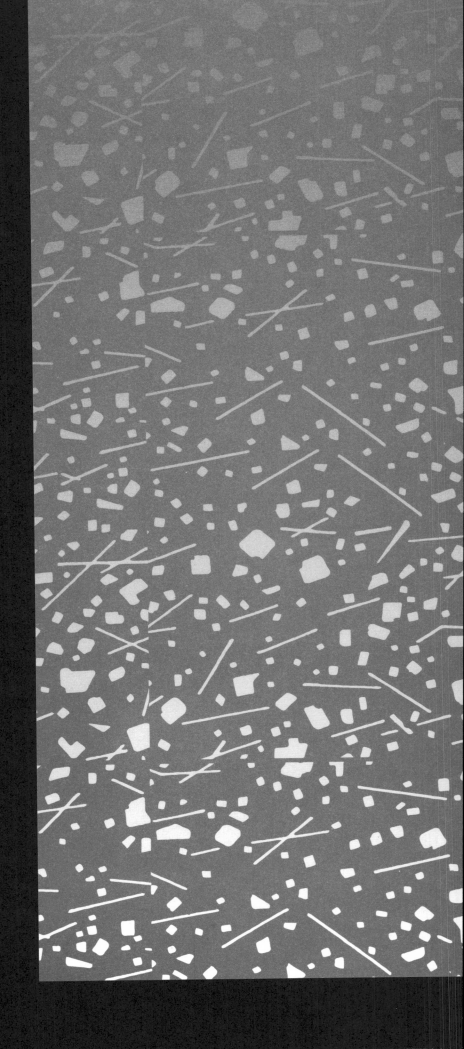

This steady composition is also seen in "Red and White Plum Blossoms" painted by Korin Ogata. His Korin School (Rin'pa) in the Edo period established a classical style of Japanese painting. This paired and balanced composition is also seen in the motifs of "Ahum" (a pair of stone-carved guardian dogs with an open mouth and a closed mouth at the gate of a Shinto shrine), a crane and a tortoise (well wishing compliments), and Emperor and Empress dolls in ancient costumes.

Red and White
Japanese Apricot
Blossoms

**KOHAKU
BAI ZU**

PAGE:86~87 | FILE FORMAT:EPS | FILE NAME:62_Tanpopo.eps

PAGE:88 | FILE FORMAT:EPS | FILE NAME:34_Kohakubai-zu.eps

Wisteria flower petals sway in the spring breeze and fall on the ground looking as if violets or dandelions are growing together. The pointillism-like color of the flowers makes a dazzlingly beautiful scene.

Spring Flowers

HARU SOKA-ZU

Fallen maple red leaves swaying in the stream make us imagine the changing stream of time.

Red Maple Leaves
in the Running Water

**RYUSUINI-
MOMIJI**

Field of Rape Blossoms
NANOHANA-BATAKE

The hazy spring field is overrun by rape blossoms. One of the Japanese rules of art uses a perspective that depict objects in the foreground as larger and objects in the back-ground as smaller.

The skirts of the mountains are beautifully decorated with a stunning brocade, but the fallen red maple leaves flowing on the running water are even more attractive.

Red Maple Leaves
in the Running Water
MOMIJI-RYUSUI

PARTS

| PAGE:90 | FILE FORMAT:EPS | FILE NAME:23_Harusouka-zu2.eps |

PARTS

| PAGE:91 | FILE FORMAT:EPS | FILE NAME:46_Ryusui-ni-momiji.eps |

PAGE:92 | FILE FORMAT:EPS | FILE NAME:40_Nanohana-batake.eps

PAGE:93 | FILE FORMAT:EPS | FILE NAME:38_Momiji-ryusui.eps

Flowering Plants in the Spring
HARUSOUKA-ZU

Violets and dandelions grow in clusters in the fields where the chattering of birds can be heard in the distance. This is a mild spring day scene.

PARTS

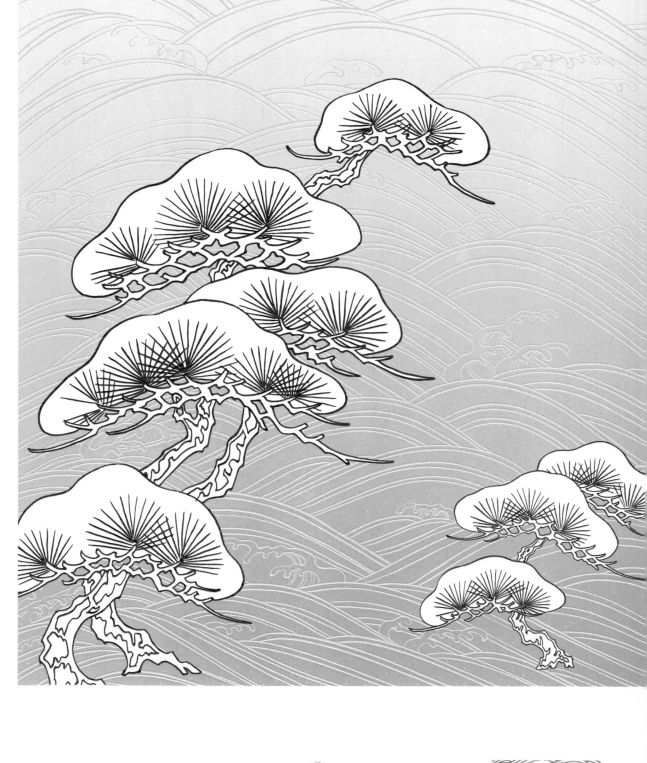

Pines are growing near the seashore with a distant sea background. The pines standing against the strong sea wind make us imagine the sound of the wind. The tea masters call the sound of the steam from the teakettle "Sho-fu", the whispering of the wind in the pines.

Wind in the Pines
SHO-FU

P A R T S

PAGE:98

FILE FORMAT:EPS

FILE NAME:54_Sho-fu.eps

Motifs are often used for folding screens. The composition perspective places peonies in the foreground and pines in the background.

P A R T S

PAGE:99

FILE FORMAT:EPS

FILE NAME:20_Harubotan-zu.eps

Spring Peonies

HARU BOTAN-ZU

The precious-metal leaves are used effectively. The sunlight of early summer and the impression reminded from the strong color of the clematis make a strong edge for the picture.

Clematis
TESSEN

Lotus
HASU

The lotus, native to India, was introduced from the Indian sub-continent long ago. The lotus appeared as a motif for statues and paintings of Buddha and is used as a symbol for Paradise. White and salmon-pink colored flowers blossom on the surface of the water in summer. The lotus roots are eaten as food.

PARTS

PAGE:100~101 | FILE FORMAT:EPS | FILE NAME:65_Tessen.eps

PARTS

PAGE:102 | FILE FORMAT:EPS | FILE NAME:25_Hasu2.eps

The hydrangeas in the rainy season change from white to purple and salmon pink. Their interspersed appearance makes us aware of the changes.

Hydrangeas
Ajisai

The background is a pattern of pools of water, and the blossoming lotus flowers are interspersed on the surface of the water. There is a strong Buddhist color because the lotus flowers are the flowers of Paradise.

Lotus
Hasu

It is said that Azami (thistle) comes from Arasashimochi (a plant with prickles) and Azamu (being amazed) because the foliage has many prickles. It is also called "mayu-zukuri (made with eyebrows)" because the hemispherical shape of the flower looks like a powder puff.

Thistles
Azami

Lilies have giant blossoms, but the composition of the pictures uses some lilies drawn together in order to stress their neat and tidy beauty.

Lily
Yuri

P A R T S

PAGE:104 | FILE FORMAT:EPS | FILE NAME:02_Ajisai2.eps

P A R T S

PAGE:105 | FILE FORMAT:EPS | FILE NAME:24_Hasu.eps

PARTS

PAGE:106 | FILE FORMAT:EPS | FILE NAME:12_Azami.eps

PARTS

PAGE:107 | FILE FORMAT:EPS | FILE NAME:72_Yuri.eps

Hydrangeas
Ajisai

Hydrangea flowers appear during the rainy season, and the flowers remind us of the humidity of early summer. The hydrangea flower is also often drawn with the motif of the snail that brings humidity with it. However, it has been said that the toxicity of the hydrangea leaves essentially keeps the snails away.

A lattice design pattern for the bamboo fence was chosen for this design of flowers symbolizing summer, Morning Glories hanging entwined on the bamboo fence.

Morning Glories on a
Latticed Window
KOSHINI-ASAGAO

The irises were well-known as a theme that the Rin'pa painters used for the four seasons. The motif uses a stream running from this side to the back to express perspective.

Irises in a stream

RYUSUINI-SHOBU

A cluster of wild chrysanthemums blossom from the earth, and flowers from a paulownia tree bloom in the sky. The composition develops space between the top and the bottom.

Autumn Flowers
AKISOKA-ZU

P A R T S

| PAGE:110 | FILE FORMAT:EPS | FILE NAME:01_Ajisai.eps |

P A R T S

| PAGE:111 | FILE FORMAT:EPS | FILE NAME:30_Khoshi-ni-asagao.eps |

 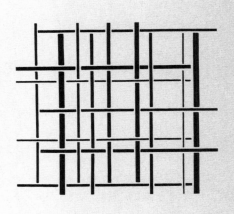

PAGE:112　　|　　FILE FORMAT:EPS　　|　　FILE NAME:47_Ryusui-ni-Shobu.eps

PAGE:113　　|　　FILE FORMAT:EPS　　|　　FILE NAME:07_Akisoka-zu.eps

The Morning Glories give a strong impression as the vine hangs down from the upper left.

Morning Glories
ASAGAO

PARTS

PAGE:116

FILE FORMAT:EPS

FILE NAME:11_Asagao.eps

Irises grow in clusters in a lake as a pair of turtle doves swim among them. The composition of the painting reproduces the nature of early summer.

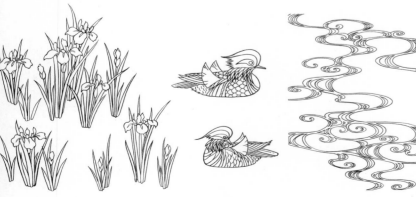

PARTS

PAGE:117

FILE FORMAT:EPS

FILE NAME:52_Shobu-ni-oshidori.eps

Turtle Doves
among the Irises

SHOBUNI-OSHIDORI

The orchids in front are drawn bigger, and the ones in the upper right are placed to make them look smaller, making you feel the depth of the picture.

Japanese Orchids

Waran

PARTS

PAGE:118

FILE FORMAT:EPS

FILE NAME:70_Waran.eps

The arrangement of irises on the precious-metal leaves. The impressed leaves play the role of water, and the growth of the irises in the pond is expressed.

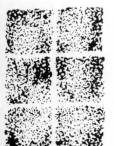

P A R T S

PAGE:119

FILE FORMAT:EPS

FILE NAME:53_Shobu.eps

Irises

SHOBU

The ears of rice lean to the left in this design that lets us feel the abundance and rhythm of the fall harvest.

Ears of rice
Inaho

The fall harvest
Aki no minori

The harvest of persimmons and chestnuts symbolizes the fall. The Japanese expression "yamano-sachi (mountain products)" shows our thankfulness for the blessings of nature.

PARTS

PARTS

  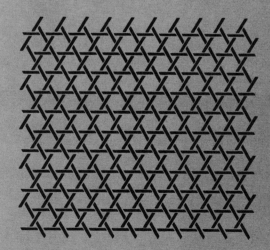

Cosmos
Akizakura

The cosmos all bloom together in the fall fields. The essence of fall is shown in the composition arranged with a single red dragon-fly known as "Aki-akane (autumnal red sunset)" on a cosmos flower.

A heavy growth of flowers on fields and mountains is arranged in this must have design.

Autumn flowers
Akikusazu

A fall garden is seen with the moonlight shining on it through this bamboo blind. The composition of the fall almost lets you hear the insects.

Moonlight in Fall
Akizuki

The chrysanthemum petals have been made big and long in this turbulent pattern. It is presented with an absolutely gorgeous pattern of flower-shaped rhombus in honey-comb.

Full-blown
Chrysanthemums
Rangiku

PARTS

PAGE:124	FILE FORMAT:EPS	FILE NAME:08_Akizakura.eps

PARTS

PAGE:125	FILE FORMAT:EPS	FILE NAME:04_Akikusazu.eps

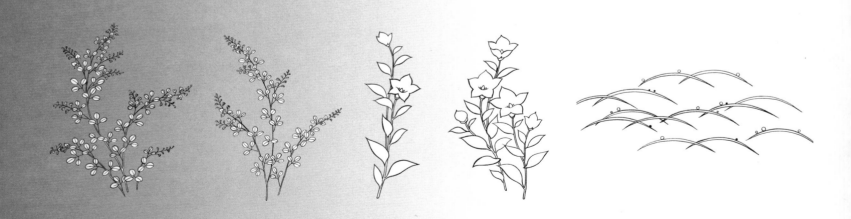

PAGE:126 | FILE FORMAT:EPS | FILE NAME:10_Akizuki.eps

PAGE:127 | FILE FORMAT:EPS | FILE NAME:45_Rangiku.eps

Magnificent full-blown chrysanthemums and small flowers make a beautiful cluster of flowers. The picture is composed of a motif of chrysanthemums with many different shapes. This kind of motif that uses a brilliant assortment of varieties of the same type is called "enumeration". It is one of the Japanese composition designs.

Enumeration of
Chrysanthemums
Kikuzukushi

PARTS

PAGE:130

FILE FORMAT:EPS

FILE NAME:31_Kikuzukushi.eps

The Japanese bush clover is arranged in the front and back to express the splendid appearance of the florettes.

PARTS

PAGE:131

FILE FORMAT:EPS

FILE NAME:19_Hagi.eps

Japanese
Bush Clover

Hagi

A slight angle is put on the Japanese pampas grass to feel the movement of the autumn breeze.

Japanese
Pampas Grass
Susuki

PARTS

PAGE:132

FILE FORMAT:EPS

FILE NAME:59_Susuki.eps

The words "abundant harvest" suit this picture as the harvest of ears of rice bend down from their heads. The sparrows flocking around the fallen ears are added to the picture and show us the fall season.

PARTS

PAGE:133

FILE FORMAT:EPS

FILE NAME:37_Minori.eps

The Harvest
Minori

Wild Chrysanthemums
Nogiku

The magnificent wild chrysanthemums are in a bold layout and present a brilliant impression.

This is an example of the composition of a design for a theme for a Japanese picture. A silhouette of blooming chrysanthemums floating on the paper sliding screen for the round window shows a typical scene of fall.

Chrysanthemums
in a Round Window
Marumado ni kiku

The scarlet maple leaves drawn
from the top to the bottom make
you feel the autumn colors even
more.

Scarlet
Maple Leaves
Momiji

Autumn flowers are a typical theme for Japanese pictures. Various autumn flowers less showy will make you think of deep Japanese aesthetics.

Autumn Flowers
Akikusa

P A R T S

PAGE:134 | FILE FORMAT:EPS | FILE NAME:43_Nogiku .eps

P A R T S

PAGE:135 | FILE FORMAT:EPS | FILE NAME:35_Marumado-ni-kiku.eps

PAGE:136 | FILE FORMAT:EPS | FILE NAME:39_Momiji.eps

PAGE:137 | FILE FORMAT:EPS | FILE NAME:03_Akikusa.eps

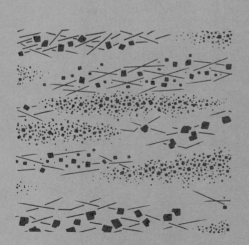

Planted in gardens, rockeries, banks, and more, preventing the earth from giving way, the sod also adds beauty. The sod grows thick and appears to be in a design tied together in the evening and morning dew.

Dew on the Sod
Tsuyushiba

P A R T S

PAGE:140

FILE FORMAT:EPS

FILE NAME:67_Tsuyushiba.eps

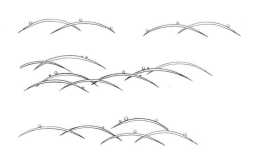

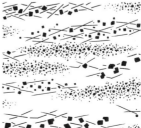

This picture uses the Indian fylfot pattern interspersed with bell flowers on a grand scale. It is a typical image of fall.

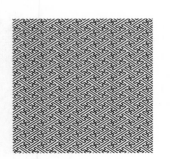

PARTS

PAGE:141

FILE FORMAT:EPS

FILE NAME:32_Kikyo.eps

Bell-flowers

Kikyo

The composition of fallen leaves of various shapes is created by the fall breeze. This is called "drifting" with the appearance of various items gathered together. The same term is used in construction for frames of paper sliding doors, latticework, rafters, and other items that are gathered together in twos and threes.

Drifting
Fukiyose

P A R T S

PAGE:142

FILE FORMAT:EPS

FILE NAME:16_Fukiyose.eps

Paulownia is a noble pattern. Long ago, it was only used by the Imperial Family, but it was a pattern that the common people dreamed of.

PARTS

PAGE:143

FILE FORMAT:EPS

FILE NAME:33_Kiri.eps

Paulownia
Kiri

Beautiful contrast between the snow covering the willow branches hanging down and the cold camellias with a vivid red and green. The stillness and the graceful power blend together into this winter scenery.

Winter Scenery
Fuyugeshiki

In this winter season there are few flowers and other colors. Clusters of crimson colored nandin (sacred bamboo) are an auspicious symbol of New Year's decorations. The sight of the winter garden along with the snow covered pine trees makes us feel the joy of New Years.

New Year's
Shogatsu

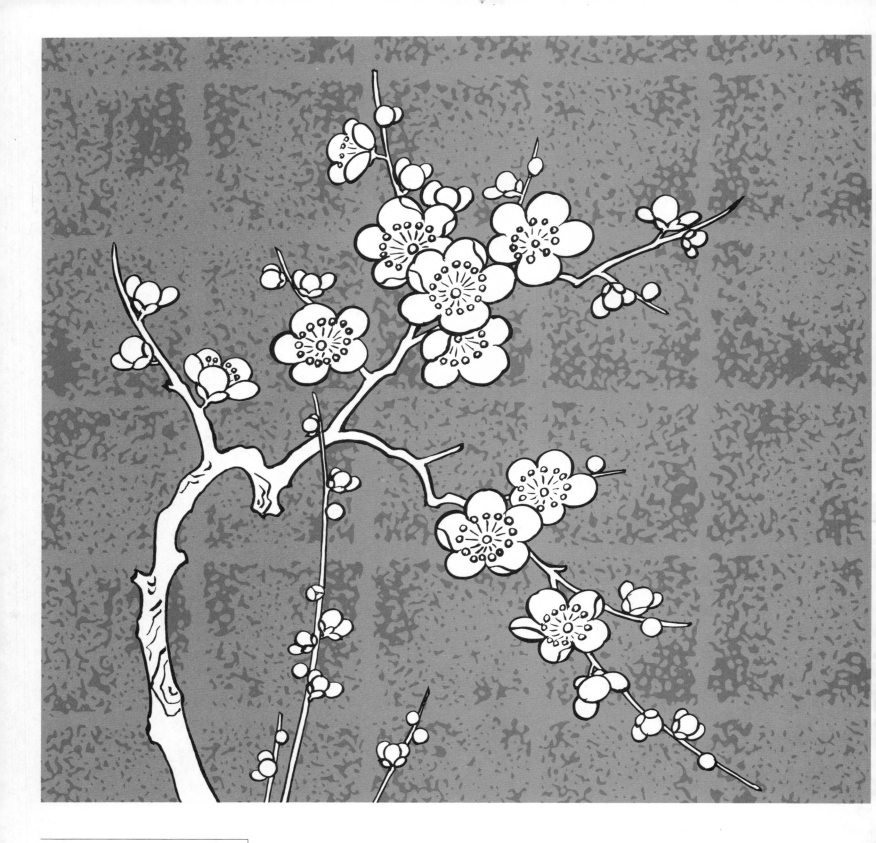

Japanese
Apricot Blossoms
Ume

Japanese apricot blossoms seen in the "Red and White Plum Blossoms" is a typical motif of the Rin'-pa artists. The blossoms have an elegance that is a little different from the cherry blossoms. The expression of blossoms with buds, not in full bloom, matches Japanese apricot blossoms.

The camellia is used as a theme from winter to spring. The flowery beauty is often used in patterns for dyeing and ceramics. The space is used consciously and the petals have been drawn large. A Japanese cypress hedge design in the background. The thin cypress boards are cut at an angle like mats.

Camellias
Tsubaki

PARTS

| PAGE:144 | FILE FORMAT:EPS | FILE NAME:18_Fuyugeshiki.eps |

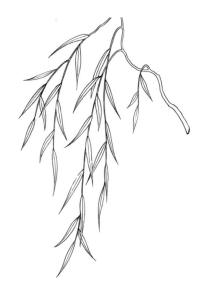  

PARTS

| PAGE:145 | FILE FORMAT:EPS | FILE NAME:55_Shogatsu.eps |

 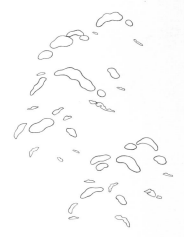 

PAGE:146 | FILE FORMAT:EPS | FILE NAME:69_Ume.eps

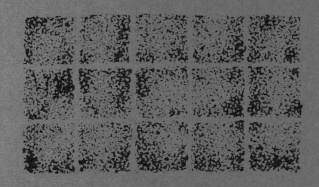

PAGE:147 | FILE FORMAT:EPS | FILE NAME:66_Tsubaki.eps

Bamboo is woven in a basket design against a background of a basket of stitches. This is a dynamic nandin layout.

Nandin

Nanten

P A R T S

PAGE:150

FILE FORMAT:EPS

FILE NAME:42_Nanten.eps

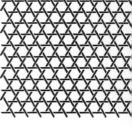

Many people see the willows around Japan. Cooling off in the evening and the rows of willow trees were very familiar to people who lived in towns. As we say, "Willows do not break under the weight of the snow". They are flexible and we use them as they can endure. They are homely, but they are what we like.

PARTS

PAGE:151

FILE FORMAT:EPS

FILE NAME:71_Yanagi.eps

Willows
Yanagi

It is the background for a quiet fall night of moonlight. Various kinds of wild flowers are collected in this composition with a motif of clustered flowers. The seven autumn flowers are Japanese bush clover, Japanese pampas grass, kudzu, dianthus, valerianaceae, eupatorium, and balloonflower.

The Seven
Autumn Flowers
**Akino-
nanakusa**

Majestic pine scenery with the sea in the background is decorated against a background of a wave design of in concentric circles.

Pine

Matsu

Pictures on the ceiling
Tenjoe-zu

This is composed of the beauties of nature painted on the ceiling, classic Japanese architectural decoration. There are many pictures painted on the ceiling. Some have a central focus and some are directionless.

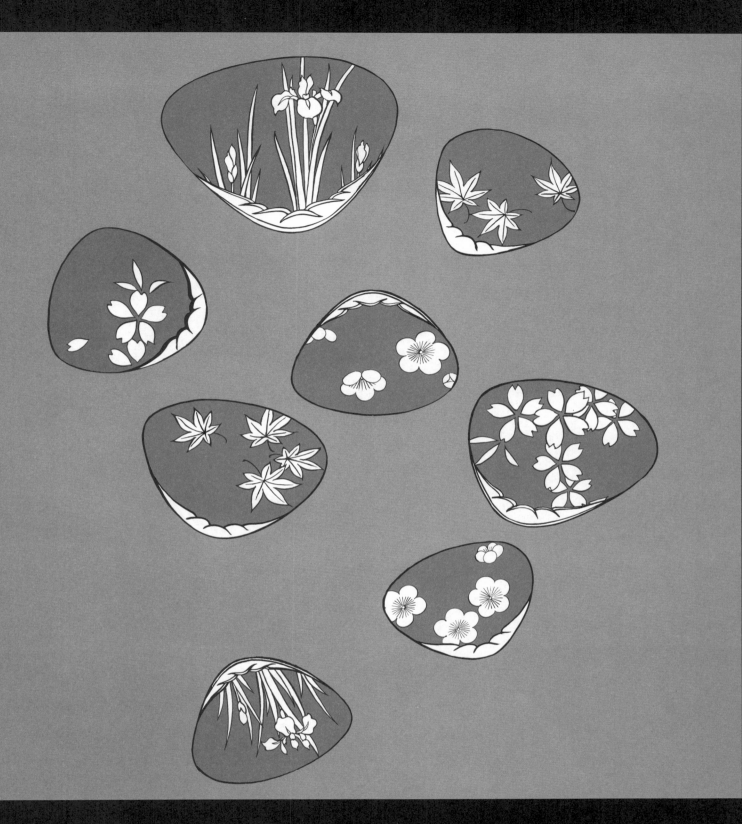

The traditional indoor amusement
motif of shell fitting is composed of
an assortment of four seasons flowers overflowing with elegance and
spirit.

Shell Fitting
Kai-awase

Scattered Folding Fans
Senmen-chirashi

Folding fans are often painted on the folding screens and sliding partitions. Various interesting pictures are playfully painted on the shapes of the folding fans. Flowers and designs of patterned pictures are gorgeously arranged on folding fans.

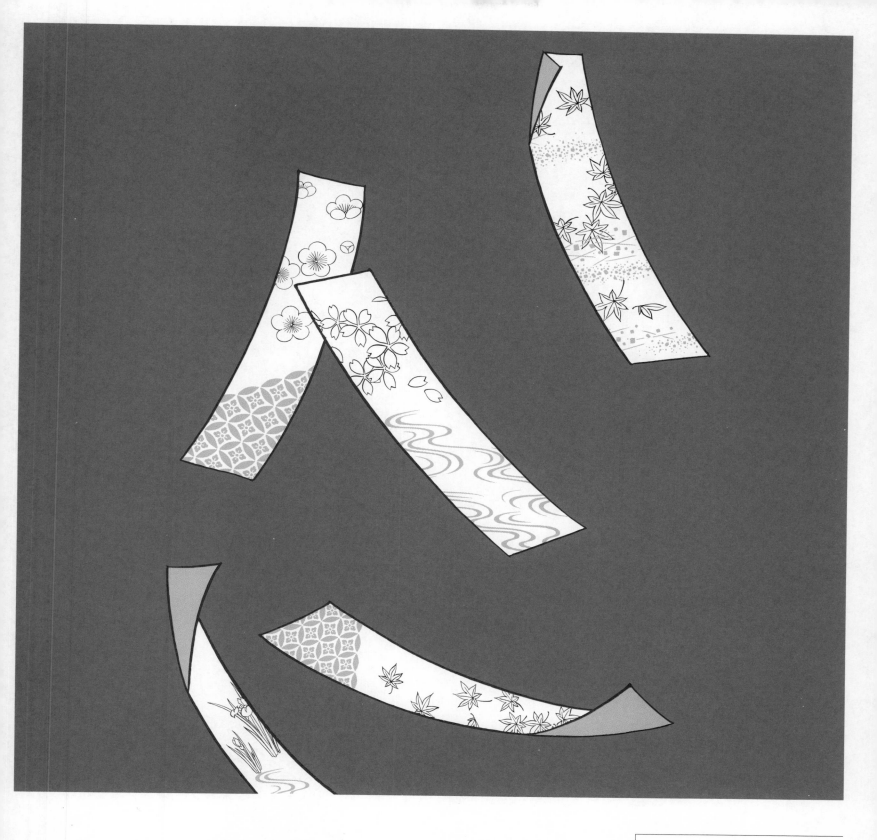

Strips of fancy paper for composing a tanka (a thirty-one syllabled poem) or haiku (a seventeen-syllabled poem) on four seasons on flutter down. This is a dynamic and gorgeous example of composition.

Scattered Fancy Strips of Paper
Tanzaku-chirashi

P A R T S

PAGE:152 | FILE FORMAT:EPS | FILE NAME:06_Akino-nanakusa.eps

P A R T S

PAGE:153 | FILE FORMAT:EPS | FILE NAME:36_Matsu.eps

PARTS

PAGE:154 | FILE FORMAT:EPS | FILE NAME:64_Tenjoe-zu.eps

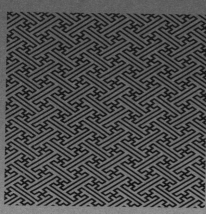

PARTS

PAGE:155 | FILE FORMAT:EPS | FILE NAME:28_Kai-awase.eps

P A R T S

PAGE:156 | FILE FORMAT:EPS | FILE NAME:50_Senmen-chirashi.eps

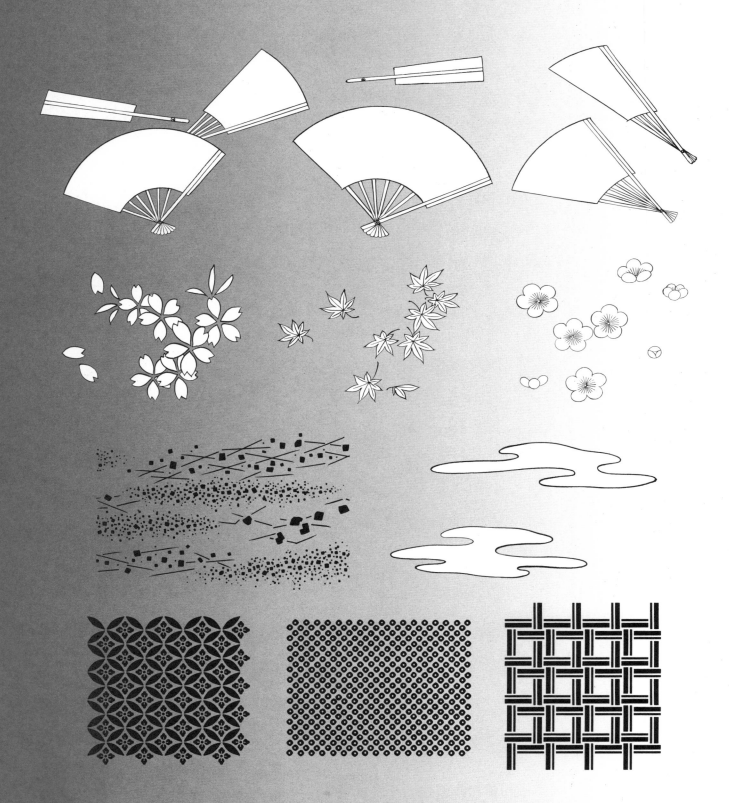

P A R T S

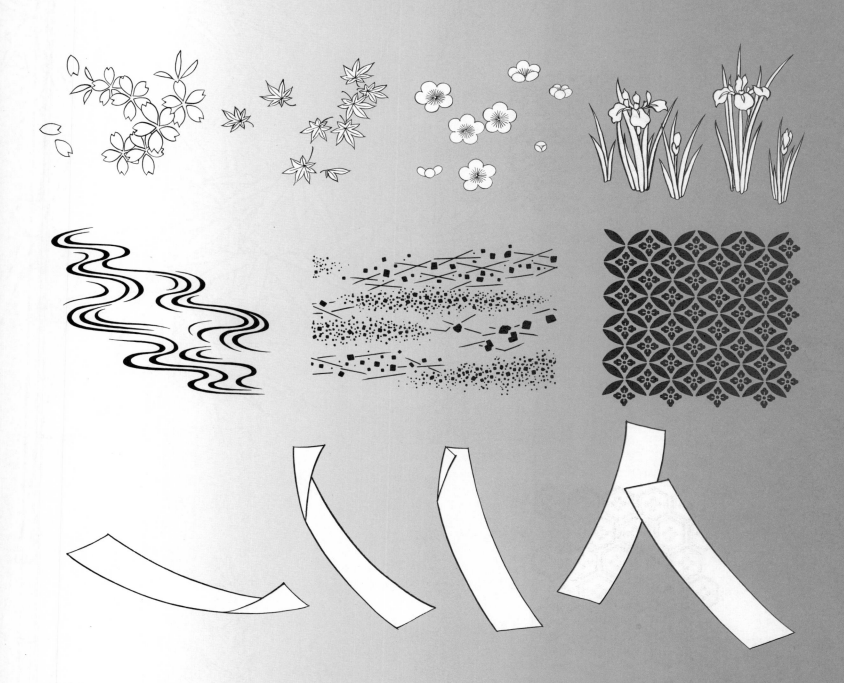

Bamboo is drawn to cut diagonally across the picture. The steadiness of the compositional arrangement has a bamboo shoot humorously coming out of the ground.

Bamboo
Take

A standing figure of beauty is prominent. Standing cranes are arranged with bamboo reaching for the sky. The compositional arrangement lets us feel action in this graceful scene.

Bamboo and Standing Crane
Takeni-tachitsuru

The gourd and vine, the background for the arabesque pattern (ivy plant pattern), have a subtle balance.

Gourd

Hyotan

The ripples are arranged in the pool of water with various flower motifs. This is a compositional arrangement that reminds us of a fantasy world from a kaleidoscope.

Flowering Pool of
Water
Soka-tamari

P A R T S

| PAGE:162 | FILE FORMAT:EPS | FILE NAME:61_Take.eps |

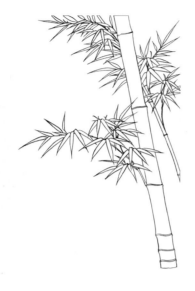  

P A R T S

| PAGE:163 | FILE FORMAT:EPS | FILE NAME:60_Take-ni-tachitsuru.eps |

P A R T S

P A R T S

The compositional arrangement shows flowers and insects as if stopped in a snapshot. We can feel the playful emotions of the artist who drew this natural motif with butterflies, praying mantises, "bell-ring" insects (highly prized for its song), bees, and other insects.

Cotton Rose

Fuyo

P A R T S

PAGE:168

FILE FORMAT:EPS

FILE NAME:17_Fuyo.eps

Appendix

The Rin'pa School

There are many themes from the Tale of Genji and dynasty classics used in Momoyama era paintings and art. Among them Koetsu Honami (1558-1637) and Sotatsu Tawaraya (dates of death and birth unknown) expressed the beauty of the dynasty through various expressive actions.

Koetsu lived together with his clan and artisans. They made works of art including calligraphy, paintings, pottery, and lacquer. Sotatsu handled art from irogami (square pieces of thick paper often used to write poems or paint pictures on), folding fans, and designs for dying and weaving to decorating buildings. Sotatsu seemed to work as a general art producer under the trade name of Tawaraya.

They were very close friends. Sotatsu painted the design for the "Anthology with Crane Design" with gold and silver paint and Koetsu Honami did the thirty-six major poets' 31-syllable Japanese poems on top. It was original and free, a refined and big-hearted work that they did together.

Sotatsu studied classical paintings, and he included his own original method of expression in the classical techniques when he drew the representative work "Wind and Thunder Gods". It is easy to imagine how his bold composition and the brilliant decorative expression of his work created a sensation.

Korin Ogata (1658-1716) was born into a family that owned a kimono fabrics (dry goods) store which was a wonderful environment to cultivate his sense of decoration. Korin learned and studied in the Kano school of painters, but then he saw Sotatsu's "Wind and Thunder Gods" and became strongly committed to that style of expression. Korin continued to search for even greater beauty with the style that Korin and Koetsu Honami developed. Korin wanted to find his own highly refined and completely new decorative expression in paintings.

His representative works "Irises"and "Red and White Plum Blossoms" are works that use sharply calculated composition which is completely different from Sotatsu's uninhibited tolerance. The motifs are realistic but subtly deformed on the layout of the works of art which result in producing beautiful folding screen art.

Hoitsu Sakai (1761-1828) completed "Summer and Autumn Grass" after taking spiritualism into the style that Sotatsu and Korin developed while getting to the bottom of spiritualism flavored with Japanese view of life as something transient and empty, modesty, and the beautiful awareness at the back of the mind. They are generally called the Rin'pa school.

The influence of the Rin'pa school went beyond the world of paintings and calligraphy. It can be seen in the decoration in the world of crafts with Korin and Kenzan's joint lacquerwork of "Lacquered Writing box with Yatsuhashi (Eight-Planked Bridge) design", including Yuzen dying, Arita and Kutani colored pictures on pottery, Kyo-yaki pottery, and Sumiya, an old meeting restaurant in Shimabara, Kyoto.

Rin'pa Chronological Table >>>

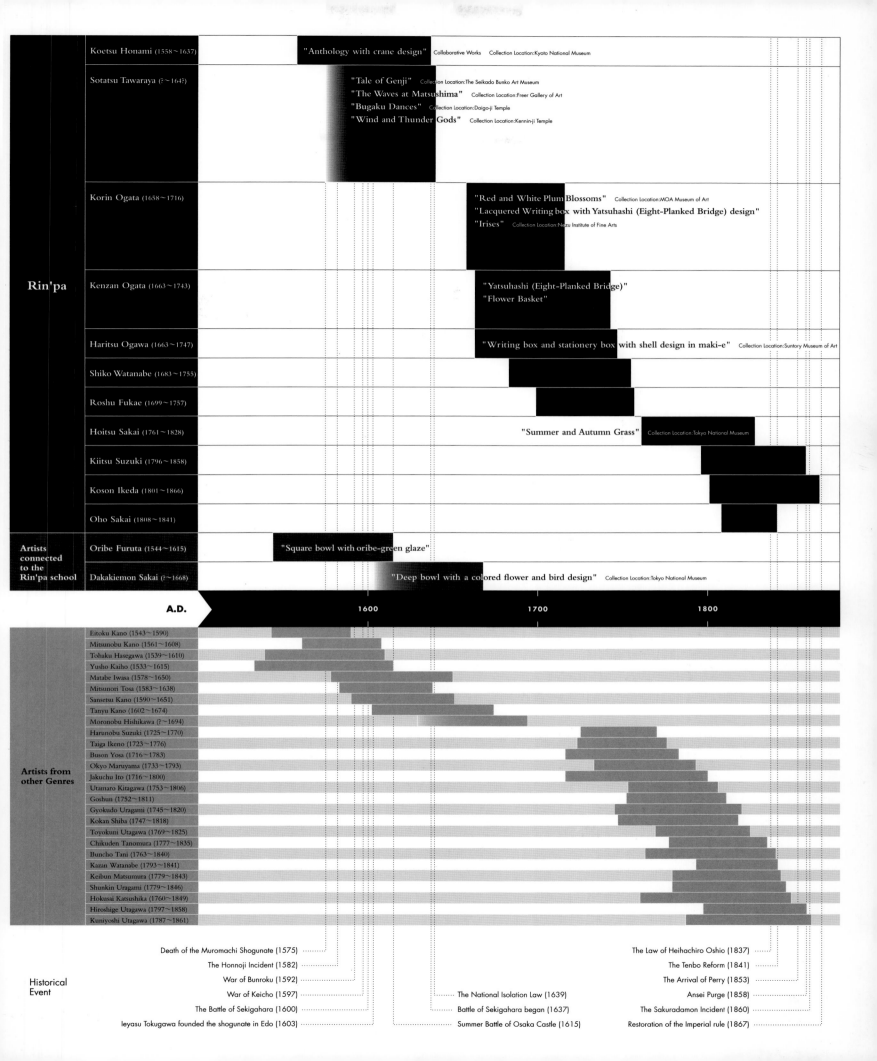

Rin'pa

Koetsu Honami (1558~1637) — "Anthology with crane design"   Collaborative Works   Collection Location:Kyoto National Museum

Sotatsu Tawaraya (?~164?)
"Tale of Genji"   Collection Location:The Seikado Bunko Art Museum
"The Waves at Matsushima"   Collection Location:Freer Gallery of Art
"Bugaku Dances"   Collection Location:Daigo-ji Temple
"Wind and Thunder Gods"   Collection Location:Kennin-ji Temple

Korin Ogata (1658~1716)
"Red and White Plum Blossoms"   Collection Location:MOA Museum of Art
"Lacquered Writing box with Yatsuhashi (Eight-Planked Bridge) design"
"Irises"   Collection Location:Nezu Institute of Fine Arts

Kenzan Ogata (1663~1743)
"Yatsuhashi (Eight-Planked Bridge)"
"Flower Basket"

Haritsu Ogawa (1663~1747) — "Writing box and stationery box with shell design in maki-e"   Collection Location:Suntory Museum of Art

Shiko Watanabe (1683~1755)

Roshu Fukae (1699~1757)

Hoitsu Sakai (1761~1828) — "Summer and Autumn Grass"   Collection Location:Tokyo National Museum

Kiitsu Suzuki (1796~1858)

Koson Ikeda (1801~1866)

Oho Sakai (1808~1841)

Artists connected to the Rin'pa school

Oribe Furuta (1544~1615) — "Square bowl with oribe-green glaze"

Dakakiemon Sakai (?~1668) — "Deep bowl with a colored flower and bird design"   Collection Location:Tokyo National Museum

A.D.   1600   1700   1800

Artists from other Genres

Eitoku Kano (1543~1590)
Mitsunobu Kano (1561~1608)
Tohaku Hasegawa (1539~1610)
Yusho Kaiho (1533~1615)
Matabe Iwasa (1578~1650)
Mitsunori Tosa (1583~1638)
Sansetsu Kano (1590~1651)
Tanyu Kano (1602~1674)
Moronobu Hishikawa (?~1694)
Harunobu Suzuki (1725~1770)
Taiga Ikeno (1723~1776)
Buson Yosa (1716~1783)
Okyo Maruyama (1733~1793)
Jakuchu Ito (1716~1800)
Utamaro Kitagawa (1753~1806)
Goshun (1752~1811)
Gyokudo Uragami (1745~1820)
Kokan Shiba (1747~1818)
Toyokuni Utagawa (1769~1825)
Chikuden Tanomura (1777~1835)
Buncho Tani (1763~1840)
Kazan Watanabe (1793~1841)
Keibun Matsumura (1779~1843)
Shunkin Uragami (1779~1846)
Hokusai Katsushika (1760~1849)
Hiroshige Utagawa (1797~1858)
Kuniyoshi Utagawa (1787~1861)

Historical Event

Death of the Muromachi Shogunate (1575)
The Honnoji Incident (1582)
War of Bunroku (1592)
War of Keicho (1597)
The Battle of Sekigahara (1600)
Ieyasu Tokugawa founded the shogunate in Edo (1603)
The National Isolation Law (1639)
Battle of Sekigahara began (1637)
Summer Battle of Osaka Castle (1615)
The Law of Heihachiro Oshio (1837)
The Tenbo Reform (1841)
The Arrival of Perry (1853)
Ansei Purge (1858)
The Sakuradamon Incident (1860)
Restoration of the Imperial rule (1867)

CD-ROM TEMPLATES INDEX

System requirement (Windows and Macintosh hybrid)

Windows:
CPU: 486
OS: MS-Windows 95 or higher
RAM: 16MB or more
Monitor: 256 colors or more, 640 x 480 pixels or higher
CD-ROM drive
Application with readable capability of EPS format files

Macintosh
CPU: Macintosh LCII series or higher version
OS: System 7.1 or higher (KanjiTalk)
RAM: 16MB or more
Monitor
Monitor: 256 colors or more, 640 x 480 pixels or higher
CD-ROM drive
Application with readable capability of EPS format files

How to Use Templates in this CD-ROM

1) Select any desirable templates from pages 174-186/template parts from pages 66-168 and confirm the file names indicated there.
2) Insert the CD-ROM to the CD-ROM in your machine and double-click the icon.
3) Search the file names you have chosen and drag the equivalent files to your desktop to copy the images.

License Agreement on "Japanese Design/Design Configuration" in CD-ROM

1. License

1) DesignEXchange Company Limited (hereinafter called "DEX") hereby grant a non-exclusive and non-transferable right and license to use "Japanese Design" in CD-ROM (hereinafter referred to as "Software") only on one computer at the same time to a customer who has purchased the Software and agreed the terms and conditions of this Agreement (hereinafter referred to as "User").

2) The User may process or edit templates, illustrations, images and other materials included in the Software (hereinafter referred to as "Materials") or distribute them in combination with other materials on a printed matter as design materials in a User's work except for the cases that fall under the following "Limitations". Provided, however, that it may be separately required to obtain a copyright of an image material (if a subject falls under a copyrightable work), design right or right of likeness, etc., depending on the use of the Materials.

2. Limitations

The User shall not
1) reproduce the Software and manual except for the cases where it is necessary to use the Software on one computer and the Materials are used under the preceding Paragraph;
2) assign to any other party the license under this Software License Agreement or permit such party to use the Software by lease or in other method;
3) disassemble or decompile whole or part of the Software;
4) manufacture or sell software products, etc., upon use of the Materials;
5) supply download service via the Internet upon use of the Materials (inclusive of greeting card service);
6) produce, sell postcards, name cards or collections of illustrations or supply the production service upon use of the Material;
7) produce, sell video shooting and editing or supply the production service upon use of the Materials;
8) use the Materials in a substantial part of such product as a postcard, calendar, or sticker;
9) use the Materials as an image that symbolizes a product or service of a specific company (Visual Identity);
10) use the Materials as a logo mark or character of a company that embodies a corporate idea (Corporate Identity); or
11) use the Materials in violation of the public order and moral or for slander and defame.

3. Copyright and other Intellectual Property Rights

Any copyright or other intellectual property rights in and to the Software and/or Materials shall not be assigned to the User. Any and all rights in connection with them shall be reserved to DEX as an exclusive property right. The User shall be deemed as granted the right and license to use the Software or Materials subject to this License Agreement on "Takumi no Hon" in CD-ROM to the limited extent of the license above.

4. Disclaimer of Warranty

The Software is offered AS IS, and any warranty shall be disclaimed as to no error, no infringement of a right of a third party and warranty of merchantability and fitness for particular purpose.

5. Limitation on Liability

DEX shall not be liable for any and all loss and disadvantage (inclusive of loss of profit and destruction of data) that may arise from the use or impossibility to use the Software and the use of the Materials irrespective of cause of a claim.

6. Termination of License

When the User has violated this Software License Agreement, DEX may terminate the license to the User under this License Agreement.

Inquiry on the Software to:

Fax: 81 3 5798 0212
E-mail: intl@dex.ne.jp
DesignEXchange Company Limited
BR Takanawa, 3-12-8, Takanawa, Minato-ku, Tokyo
108-0074, Japan
(To ensure the proper guidance to your inquiry, please help us to receive the written messages only by fax or by e-mail.)

FILE FORMAT:EPS
FILE NAME:T01_Ajisai.eps

FILE FORMAT:EPS
FILE NAME:T02_Ajisai2.eps

FILE FORMAT:EPS
FILE NAME:T03_Akikusa.eps

FILE FORMAT:EPS
FILE NAME:T04_Akikusazu.eps

FILE FORMAT:EPS
FILE NAME:T05_Akino-minori.eps

FILE FORMAT:EPS
FILE NAME:T06_Akino-nanakusa.eps

FILE FORMAT:EPS
FILE NAME:T07_Akisoka-zu.eps

FILE FORMAT:EPS
FILE NAME:T08_Akizakura.eps

FILE FORMAT:EPS
FILE NAME:T09_Akizakura2.eps

FILE FORMAT:EPS
FILE NAME:T10_Akizuki.eps

FILE FORMAT:EPS
FILE NAME:T11_Asagao.eps

FILE FORMAT:EPS
FILE NAME:T12_Azami.eps

FILE FORMAT:EPS
FILE NAME:T13_Botan.eps

FILE FORMAT:EPS
FILE NAME:T14_Fuji.eps

FILE FORMAT:EPS
FILE NAME:T15_Fujidana.eps

FILE FORMAT:EPS

FILE FORMAT:EPS

FILE FORMAT:EPS

FILE FORMAT:EPS
FILE NAME:T19_Hagi.eps

FILE FORMAT:EPS
FILE NAME:T20_Harubotan-zu.eps

FILE FORMAT:EPS
FILE NAME:T21_Harukaze.eps

FILE FORMAT:EPS
FILE NAME:T22_Harusouka-zu.eps

FILE FORMAT:EPS
FILE NAME:T23_Harusouka-zu2.eps

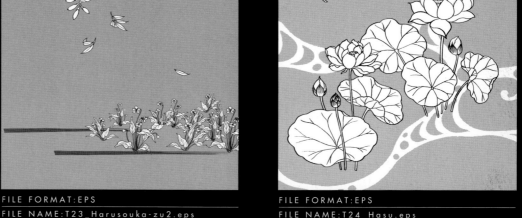

FILE FORMAT:EPS
FILE NAME:T24_Hasu.eps

FILE FORMAT:EPS
FILE NAME:T25_Hasu2.eps

FILE FORMAT:EPS
FILE NAME:T26_Hyotan.eps

FILE FORMAT:EPS
FILE NAME:T27_Inaho.eps

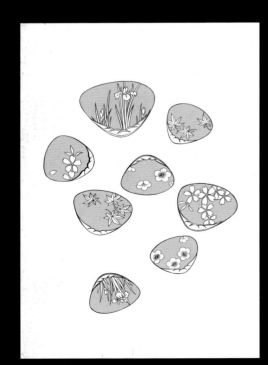

FILE FORMAT:EPS
FILE NAME:T28_Kai-awase.eps

FILE FORMAT:EPS
FILE NAME:T29_Kaika-zu.eps

FILE FORMAT:EPS
FILE NAME:T30_Khoshi-ni-asagao.eps

FILE FORMAT:EPS
FILE NAME:T31_Kikuzukushi.eps

FILE FORMAT:EPS
FILE NAME:T32_Kikyo.eps

FILE FORMAT:EPS
FILE NAME:T33_Kiri.eps

FILE FORMAT:EPS

FILE FORMAT:EPS

FILE FORMAT:EPS

FILE FORMAT:EPS
FILE NAME:T37_Minori.eps

FILE FORMAT:EPS
FILE NAME:T38_Momiji-ryusui.eps

FILE FORMAT:EPS
FILE NAME:T39_Momiji.eps

FILE FORMAT:EPS
FILE NAME:T40_Nanohana-batake.eps

FILE FORMAT:EPS
FILE NAME:T41_Nanohana.eps

FILE FORMAT:EPS
FILE NAME:T42_Nanten.eps

FILE FORMAT:EPS
FILE NAME:T43_Nogiku .eps

FILE FORMAT:EPS
FILE NAME:T44_Ohkabyobue-zu.eps

FILE FORMAT:EPS
FILE NAME:T45_Rangiku.eps

FILE FORMAT:EPS
FILE NAME:T46_Ryusui-ni-momiji.eps

FILE FORMAT:EPS
FILE NAME:T47_Ryusui-ni-Shobu.eps

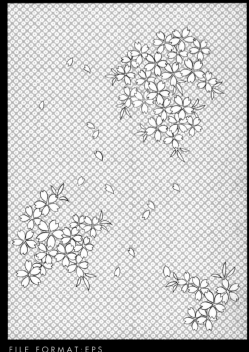

FILE FORMAT:EPS
FILE NAME:T48_Sakura-chirashi.eps

FILE FORMAT:EPS
FILE NAME:T49_Sakura.eps

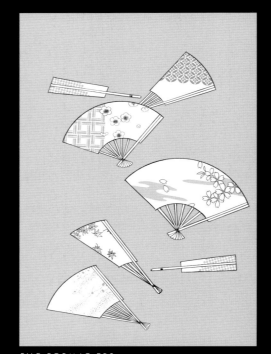

FILE FORMAT:EPS
FILE NAME:T50_Senmen-chirashi.eps

FILE FORMAT:EPS
FILE NAME:T51_Shidarezakura.eps

FILE FORMAT:EPS

FILE FORMAT:EPS

FILE FORMAT:EPS

FILE FORMAT:EPS
FILE NAME:T55_Shogatsu.eps

FILE FORMAT:EPS
FILE NAME:T56_Soka-tamari.eps

FILE FORMAT:EPS
FILE NAME:T57_Suisen.eps

FILE FORMAT:EPS

FILE FORMAT:EPS

FILE FORMAT:EPS

FILE FORMAT:EPS
FILE NAME:T61_Take.eps

FILE FORMAT:EPS
FILE NAME:T62_Tanpopo.eps

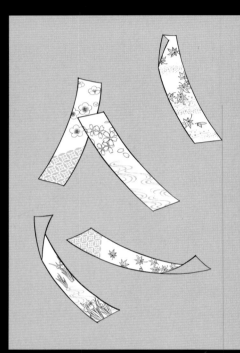

FILE FORMAT:EPS
FILE NAME:T63_Tanzaku-chirashi.eps

FILE FORMAT:EPS
FILE NAME:T64_Tenjoe-zu.eps

FILE FORMAT:EPS
FILE NAME:T65_Tessen.eps

FILE FORMAT:EPS
FILE NAME:T66_Tsubaki.eps

FILE FORMAT:EPS
FILE NAME:T67_Tsuyushiba.eps

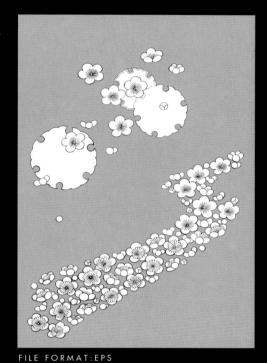

FILE FORMAT:EPS
FILE NAME:T68_Ume-ryusui.eps

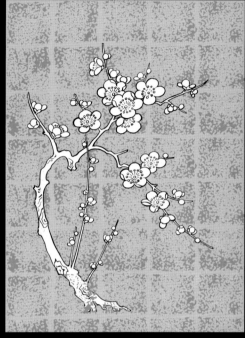

FILE FORMAT:EPS
FILE NAME:T69_Ume.eps

FILE FORMAT:EPS
FILE NAME:T70_Waran.eps

FILE FORMAT:EPS
FILE NAME:T71_Yangi.eps

FILE FORMAT:EPS
FILE NAME:T72_Yuri.eps

FILE FORMAT:EPS
FILE NAME:T73_Moyo1.eps

FILE FORMAT:EPS
FILE NAME:T74_Moyo2.eps

FILE FORMAT:EPS
FILE NAME:T75_Moyo3.eps

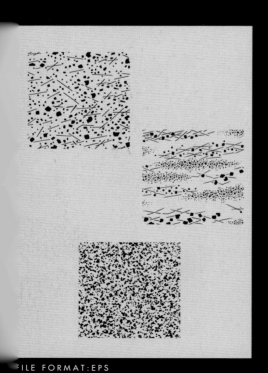

FILE FORMAT:EPS

FILE FORMAT:EPS

FILE FORMAT:EPS

INDEX

Acknowledgements

Modern day things and traditional designs can work together in harmony to make new images. Do they actually exist or do they belong to the Rin'pa school as a Yuzen design that young people have freely turned into a digital design to use? Is a new style of design being born or is it possible that traditional techniques and tools are being used to make the most of modern times and dream of new things? This book has been produced thinking of various things.

Many people were very helpful and cooperated to talk about the purposes of collecting materials and planning. I would like to thank these people from the bottom of my heart.

Thanks to Yoshimura and Hori of Nostalgic Japan who have been with us since the start of this project, to Suzuki of Fontage who has taken care of the entire project and has redone everything from the design to the digital data, to Kojima, the author and dyer who gave us advice on producing the templates, to Hashimoto, Kuwabara, and Koyanagi of Hotel Okura who cooperated with us for taking pictures of the traditional designs that were made suitable for modern use at the Hotel Okura, to Watanabe the photographer, to Yamamoto of public relations at Mizuno, Inc, Ikeda, and Hosokawa for the Aloha shirts design and doing their very best for production, to Kato of the design office, Katsuhiro Mizuno for his photography, and to Emiko Yoshise for helping with the production. We could not have done it without you. Thank you very much.

Masanori Omae

Contributors' List

Nostalgic Japan [http://www.nj-kyoto.co.jp]

Fontage [http://www.fontage.co.jp]

Hotel Okura [http://www.hotelokura.co.jp]

Mizuno Corporation Limited

Michiko Takagi

Sensho Kojima

Watanabe Studio

Mai COLLECTION [http://www.maicollection.co.jp]

Keisui Yamazaki